# The experiment that is India - II

# – a collection of fifteen essays on the globalizing Indian labour market.

# Index

<u>**Description:**</u>

This book, "The experiment that is India - II", has fifteen essays. These are not necessarily interlinked, but as it is rightly said in Social Sciences, no one issue operates in vacuum. Thus, we can understand the meteoric rise of multidisciplinary; and interdisciplinary studies, since it is of particular importance in today's day and age. The objective of selecting these particular essays is to provide a concise yet comprehensive understanding of various issues plaguing the Indian society. Extensive research and literature reference has been carried out in each essay. The language used is lucid, simple, and occasionally academic to have everlasting impact on the readers. The author has also tried to add a personal touch to the writing process wherever possible.

"The experiment that is India" Series, will try to look into this behemoth democracy of 1.32 billion people (latest figures). Although, there has been considerable economic growth the fruits of development are yet to reach the people. Only a handful of individuals still control almost the entire swathes of resources, even though Article 38 and 39 of the Indian constitution prescribe against hoarding and accumulation of resources. This is non-justiciable since it is included in Part IV of the Constitution of India, the Directive Principles of State Policy, and would require enabling legislation to see any meaningful impact on the ground. However, such legislations are yet to see the light of day. Reasons could be attributed to vested interests of policy makers, influence that these individuals hold on various corridors of power, or might be the sheer lack of political will. Furthermore, most often than not the political class has operated in cahoots with such individuals to further oppress the peoples. This has led to a structure being created which has the least concern for the common citizen.

The essays would try to shed some light on such issues. It would also bring to the forefront the paradoxes existing therein, like, smartphones with internet, but no electricity (nearly 240 million Indians still do not have electricity); houses, but no toilets (open defecation); the audacity of a loan defaulter with outstanding loan of close to Rs. 90 billion (Rs. 9000 crore) comfortably living in the serene suburbs close to London, and the numerous farmers committing suicide because of the inability to repay, or borrow paltry sums. The author also understands many worrisome ground realities like, how comfortable rural middle class families may fall into the vicious cycle of poverty just with the occurrence of a single medical episode in the family. Since, private medical care is atrociously expensive and although medical insurance is an option, most often than not the individual and the family has to inevitably foot a huge portion of the bills. And the government medical infrastructure is in shambles. With such understandings and research this book will try to provide the readers with an unique, and authentic understanding of the contemporaneous societal issues in India.

**About the author:**

 Swarnava Sayan Bhadra is a Graduate "B.A. (S.S.)" (2014-17) of the Tata Institute of Social Sciences, Hyderabad; and "M.A. (G.L.)" (2017-19), T.I.S.S., Mumbai. He is 23 years old, and was born in the city of joy, Kolkata. He has done a major part of his schooling from Bangalore. He has studied at Army Public School, Bangalore; Rashtriya Military School, Bangalore; and various Kendriya Vidyalayas. He is a professional who wants to bring about positive change in the world.

His long term goal is to have a nationwide chain of animal shelters where all abandoned and stray animals would be brought and given a respectable life. He plans to do this with a cooperative sustainable mode of operation, in which he would employ destitute, and vagrants. As employees they will be entitled to decent housing, medical facilities, and other such benefits to live a dignified life. He sincerely hopes that someday he is able to eradicate homelessness, begging, and poverty.

He believes in the philosophy of "Vasudhaiva Kutumbakam", which translates to, "The world is one family". He yearns for a peaceful and just world.

This book is his attempt towards creating something meaningful and worthy.

## Preface:

"They alone live who live for others" – Swami Vivekananda

Dear Readers,

Right at the onset let me proclaim something, I love my country. Period. This line is important because in some of the essays it might seem like I detest this land. But that is absolutely not the case.

The field of Social Sciences is such that it inevitably antagonizes the state and its machinery. For instance (but not limited to) the existing government in power, erstwhile governments, societal structures, etc. But, this criticism for the governments, prevailing structures and systems, should not be misconstrued as acrimony towards the nation. If the Social Scientists are not able to exasperate the government, then frankly, they are failing miserably at their prescribed job.

A mature state is that which understands this, and works in harmony with all the ensuing critiques. A nation is made of its people and governed by the constitution, which is sacrosanct, this must never be forgotten; as Mark Twain once famously remarked, "Loyalty to the country always; loyalty to the government when it deserves it".

India today is the largest practicing democracy in the world. Although, it was envisaged to be a "welfare state", it seems to have been wretchedly unsuccessful at that. I would like to call it an un-ideal experiment. Perhaps

India was the only country which gave all its citizens equal universal adult franchisee right at the dawn of independence; but could not give economic justice. The preamble clearly states the founding ideals of this great nation, justice of social, economic, and political; liberty; equality of status, and opportunity; and fraternity, assuring the dignity of the human, and unity of the nation. Even though these were the founding principles of the Indian state, there remains a huge way to traverse before realizing this egalitarian dream.

I have always firmly believed in the sayings, "The world is not changed by your opinion, but by your example, and actions" - Paulo Coelho, and, "Be the change you wish to see in the world" - Mahatma Gandhi. This has to be the mantra of the youth. We should not let our demographic dividend turn into a demographic disaster. We have to find a solution to the present phenomenon of jobless growth.

At this juncture, I would like to quote a Bengali song "aami ek jajabar" ("I am a wanderer"), by Bhupen Hazarika, in which there is a very powerful line, "aami dekhechi onek gogonchumbi ottalikar shari; tar chayatai dekhechi anek, grihohin noro-nari". Which translates to, "I have seen a lot of swanky high-rises, and in its shadow a lot of homeless, destitute people".

This holds a tremendous amount of contemporary relevance. The present socio-economic milieu is abundant with such blatant instances of inequality rampantly plaguing our country, and the world. There is a pertinent need to work towards finding solutions to this, and providing a humane and dignified life for all our people.

No discussion about society and country can be without involving the polity prevailing in it. The political realm is of prime importance, especially in a democratic setup like India. Karl Marx once said, "From each according to their ability, to each according to their need". I am in no way a "Marxist". Furthermore, I find it increasingly difficult to concur with the arm-chair Marxists. They do not resonate with me; neither does the "nationalistic" right wing. And the saddest part of it all is that the only centrist party in India is nothing more than the manifestation of all that is wrong with the country, hence I despise it to the core. Thus, I find it increasingly difficult to reconcile with any of the mainstream political parties. The left-wingers accuse me of being right, and the right wingers accuse me of being left. So sometimes it can get really confusing for me. Some of the political thinkers who appeal greatly to me are Netaji S. C. Bose, Dr. B. R. Ambedkar, Bhagat Singh, and other such leaders of the same integrity level.

More than any ideology I believe in principles of honesty, humanity, character, competence, integrity, democracy, logic, trust, empathy and rationality. If I have to create an amalgamation of these from various ideologies, so be it. I supremely loathe hypocrisy, rigidity, regressive attitudes, partisanship, divisiveness, malevolent profiteering, and exploitative practices.

Be it my professional, or personal life I strictly adhere to these principles.

I hope you like my book. :) :)

Feedbacks and criticisms are always welcome. :)


Swarnava Sayan Bhadra

10th/ Feb/ 2019

Mumbai, India.

## 1st. The persistence of Child Labour – an abhorring reality

<u>**List of abbreviations**</u>

| BIMARU | Bihar, Madhya Pradesh, Rajasthan, and Uttar Pradesh |
|--------|----------------------------------------------------|
| EU | European Union |
| ILO | International Labour Organization |
| UNICEF | The United Nations Children's Fund |
| US | United States |

**Introduction:**

"Child labour perpetuates poverty, unemployment, illiteracy, and other social evils."

– Kailash Satyarthi

According to the ILO in the year 1990 there were 79 million "child labour" (Mukherjee & Das, 2008; Bhukuth, 2008; Maurya, 2001) in the world (Basu & Van, 1998); in the year 2013 this figure stood at 265 million (Ospina & Roser, 2017). The child labour force in India has been estimated at around 4.3 million by the 2011 Census, and 10.1 million by UNICEF (Umapathy, 2017). These differences in the total estimation occur because of many reasons including underreporting, and varied technicalities in definitions (Chandrasekhar & Ghosh, 2007).

The term "child labour" is defined as children between the ages of 5-14 engaged in economic activities and working on a part or full time basis (Doepke & Zilibotti, 2009). Child labour constitutes 13% of the total labour force in India. The total number of child labour has also increased in the urban areas according to the 2001 and 2011 Census reports from 1.3 million to 2 million (Ospina & Roser, 2017). Also, child labour has been increasingly associated with "invisibility". This has happened because of a changing pattern in the location of work from factories to the homes and private spaces of business owners and employers (Basu & Tzannatos, 2003).

Article 24 of the Indian Constitution, which is a fundamental right, prohibits employment of children in factories, mines, and other hazardous industries (Sumanta, 1980), which at present includes mining, explosives, and occupations listed in the Factories Act, 1948. However, employment in non-hazardous industries was not explicitly banned, until recently, and thus provides a lot of scope for exploitation because of the existence of grey areas in the legalities (Lieten, 2002). The Child Labour (Prohibition and Abolition) Act of 1986 was aimed at identifying, prosecuting, and thus putting an end to child labour in India (Basu, 2003).

Child Labour (Prohibition and Prevention) Amendment Act, 2016 puts a complete ban on child labour, below 14 years of age; and bans adolescents, between 14 – 18 years, in hazardous industries (Ministry of Law, GOI).

## Part I

"Poverty is the worst form of violence"

– Mahatma Gandhi

Poverty is considered to be the primary reason behind children being forced into work (Pande, 1996). In some families the income from children constitute anywhere between 25% - 40% of the total household income (Togunde & Weber, 2007; Rao & Rao, 1998). Lack of resources to attain education has been identified as another major cause behind child labour (Kovasevic, 2007). The Indian government tried to remedy this by introducing the Right to Education Act, a compulsory education policy enshrined as a Fundamental Right in the Constitution. However, even this policy is not able to meaningfully deal with the problem of child labour (DC & Wind, 2009).

Picture – 1 – Silver cooking pot factory

(Source: Geralt Novak)

Some of the states with the highest number of child labour are Uttar Pradesh (2.1 million), Bihar (1 million), Rajasthan (0.84 million), Madhya Pradesh and Maharashtra (0.7 million each) (Ospina & Roser, 2017). Child labour is also intrinsically linked with various socio, economic, and political circumstances, and vested interests. All these states fall under the classification of "BIMARU" states (except Maharashtra), as coined by Ashish Bose in the mid-1980s, this shows that the education crises in these states have also impacted in high child labour incidences.

A study involving 1535 parents and child labour was conducted by Togunde and Weber (2007). The major cause as identified by them was poverty and the need of future training for careers. Also, an astounding 88.6% of these parents had themselves worked as child labourers while growing up. Thus, there exists a vicious cycle of resource poverty which perpetuates child labour, often intergenerational. 31% of the children believe that their kids would also have to be involved in child labour to enable the financial viability of the household. With the increase in parental education the incidence of child labour decreases drastically. Child labour is more prevalent and gory especially in the less developed nations.

Children are employed, despite legal persecutions, because of the paltry wages they work for. Children work for as low as $1/5^{th}$ of the amount given to adults. They are also unaware of their rights and hence do not create problems for the employers (Braun, 2006; Rao & Rao, 1998). Child labourers are exposed to a variety of irreversible damages including, but not limited to, physical, psychological, and developmental (Iversen & Ghorpade, 2011). Their overall health, well-being, and growth are stunted (Emerson & Knabb, 2013).


**<u>Part II</u>**

"Despite the economic advantage to firms that employ child labour, it is in the social interest, as a national policy, to abolish it."

– Barry Commoner

With increasing awareness amongst buyers, international pressures, and advocacy, global corporations have been trying to do away with child labour, at least on paper (Braun, 2006). This leads to greater engagement of child labour in the informal sector and further scope for exploitation. There is a need for consciousness among the corporations to have a child labour free supply chain. The global production networks have to be sanitised for a child labour free production process. Since, in the present conditions, the production processes are extensively outsourced and subcontracted; child labour is still rampantly employed, completely unabated (Busse & Braun, 2004).

Picture – 2 – Shoe polishing

(Source: Millennium India Education Foundation)

Children are employed in a variety of manual works mostly unskilled, domestic labour specially in family owned spaces, agricultural sector, glass industries like bangles, match box making, brass and lock industries, beedi making, rag picking, embroidery, carpet making, fireworks production, mining, quarrying, brick kilns, and tea gardens (Basu, 2003). In urban areas the most widespread is the employment of child labour in the food stalls and restaurants, the quintessential "chotu". Child labour burden is also often gendered. Girls are expected to do most of the domestic and home-based work, which is often unpaid (Burra, 2001). Boys are primarily employed in wage labour outside the house (Das & Mukherjee, 2007).

Picture – 3 – Intricate embroidery work

(Source: Livemint)

Picture – 4 – The "Chotu" at work

(Source: NavBharat Times)

Directly documenting the experiences of child labour and getting accurate information about their working conditions, wages, timings, etc. proves to be one of the biggest challenges (Kovasevic, 2007). Since almost the entirety of the child labour force is employed in the informal sector it is further difficult to gather reliable information. The children are too scared to talk and the employers are too intimidated by outside interference. In general there is awareness that children must not be employed as workers, but there is also a general fearlessness that nothing concrete is going to happen. A simple lie about the age of the child is enough. Almost any child labour when asked their age would reply "16 or 17 years". Although, 1908, a nation-wide toll free number exists for reporting instances of child labour, the approach is often lackadaisical. Also, the actual child labourers on the field pose a simple question, even to genuinely concerned individuals, "how will we eat and feed our families if we start going to school?" This is a truly confrontational situation.

Since the phenomenon of child labour is multifarious in nature, there is no one way strategy to solve the problem. It requires committed action from various stakeholders, most importantly the government. Bringing financial stability at homes can be one of the entry points to start with the eradication process of child labour. Education is another such entry point (Weiner, 1996). Expanding the educational base, curbing any violence at schools, providing quality, affordable, and universal education can help provide conducive learning, schooling and overall growth environment for children. Vocational training is another mechanism to train the child labourers to have meaningful careers and lives (Maurya, 2001).

Picture – 5 – Overlapping layers of marginalization

(Source: Geralt Nowak)

Child labour also jeopardizes the future of the children involved by completely ruining the foundational aspects of childhood (Pande, 1996). This has severe repercussions for the society at large, since their chances of becoming positively productive adults diminishes considerably. Countries like India, Pakistan, Bangladesh, and majority of the Sub-Saharan countries are specifically at higher risk. Furthermore, the government educational facilities in all these countries are so abysmal that the chances of any actual upward socio-economic mobility are uncomfortably close to none. Thus, when the parents make a comparative trade-off between the sacrifices required for schooling and the probable benefits, it is a clear choice that they make. Many studies have also elucidated this, as to how many children drop out of school to work because of the inferior quality of education (Mukherjee & Das, 2008). Bourdieu (1986) interestingly initiated the idea of social and cultural capital along with economic capital. Thus, the absence of any of these three can be a contributing factor towards prevalence of child labour in the family.

Basu and Van (1998) have refuted the problematizing of parents as perpetrators of child labour. They have elicited a model in which higher adult wages automatically lead to the extinction of child labour without any bans. However, the empirical evidence for this is missing and it also discounts the fact that many child labourers might not have parents.

They might be living with their relatives or foster parents, who most often than not, in the Indian and less developed countries' context are actually abusive. Therefore, a total ban on child labour might not be the answer, as claimed by Basu and Van, but it can be one of the plausible steps to explore. However, it has to be complemented by various other protection mechanisms like educational and residential facilities for the rescued children.

In a study involving 239120 children spread over 221 districts in 18 developing nations, Webbink, Smits, and Jong (2013) found that 30-50% of children in African countries are involved in child labour, compared to the 4-10% in India and Bangladesh. A comprehensive analysis framework for understanding child labour has been used involving resources, structures, culture, rural vs. urban. The major results they found were that the children were less vulnerable to take up employment if their households were resource sufficient. If the mother is involved in low paying jobs then the children also often participate as non-wage child labour. The family disparities also play a role in this, girls work more than their male siblings; the workload also increases as the size of the family grows.

Picture – 6 – Hazardous work – firecrackers manufacturing

(Source: ILO)

Iversen and Ghorpade (2011) have studied the work-life histories of 90 individuals who migrated for work before attaining 15 years of age. The period of migration studied is from 1935-2005. Almost all the individuals narrated their experiences of being a child labour before the advent of increased awareness and the lives they had lived. Almost, all of them had to go through extremely gruesome work conditions to afford regular meals.

All of them were employed in the lowest paying jobs, and promotions were very rare. Thus, it proved to be an inexorable cycle of never ending poverty and resource scarcity.

If we consider families owning land, the incidence of child labour decreases only after a certain threshold point. The ownership of land is a sign of wealth, especially in rural areas. The land owning pattern can be divided into three categories: marginal, small, and large. The incidences of child labour increases from marginal to small land ownerships; but decreases drastically for large land owning households. In China the child labour participation rate declined from 48% in 1950 to 12% in 1995 (Basu, 2003).

Picture – 7 – "Home based" embroidery work

(Source: Frontline)

## Part III

During our field visits to Cheetah Camp, Mankhurd, and Dharavi, we could not overtly see any child labourers working in the manufacturing units. The few children that we did manage to see were too careful about what they revealed to us. Almost, all of them claimed to be "18 years old". All of them denied working in these sweatshops, and claimed that they were only visiting relatives. This illustrates their knowledge about the ban on child labour and the legalities of it. However, this is not true in many of the small food stalls in semi-urban or rural areas. Many shops even in urban areas employ children. Restaurants in Chembur have child labour working as employees, since these are non-hazardous, they even work as waiters. This is particularly worrisome. Nobody would willingly want to become a child labour; this shows a greater malaise in the society. As an envisaged "welfare state", India has not been able to provide economic opportunities for the parents of these adults, neither has it been able to provide appropriate educational and employment opportunities for these youth. The demographic dividend is soon turning into a demographic disaster, which is also visible on the ground. Suddenly in the past few years, a lot of low paying jobs are being taken up by youngsters. This is a visible trend. A lot of middle aged labourers are being replaced with a young labour force. This shows the appalling condition of our employment generation schemes. Almost all of these jobs are extremely low paying, mostly capable of providing only hand-to-mouth existence. Child labourers are paid even lesser.

## Conclusion

"You can't regulate child labour. You can't regulate slavery. Some things are just wrong."
– Michael Moore

There is no easy solution towards eradicating the problem of child labour. The legislations, bans, fundamental rights, all have been tried and all have failed to solve this in its entirety. Thus, there is a need for sustainable global production networks. Confluence between the law and market may be able to provide effective solutions. Millions of childhoods are lost to attain two square meals a day. Close to 8 million children are entrapped in debt bondage, coerced military duty, sexual slavery, etc. These criminalities can be expunged by using a strong law and order machinery. The developed U.S. and E.U. account for almost 0.5 million of these children (Basu, 2003). Trafficking of close to 1.2 million children each year is truly a blot on humanity (Basu, 2003; Webbink et al., 2013). However, problematizing child labour without taking into consideration the extreme economic and social marginalization of these families can turn out to be extremely erroneous and counterproductive (Iversen & Ghorpade, 2011).

Thus, the problem of child labour has to be solved by considering the multifarious aspects involved with it, including, but not limited to, familial structures, economic relations, social norms, marginalization, government policies, international discourses. Only by meaningfully engaging with these, child labour can be located in the intersectional marginalities. The structural inefficiencies and inequitable growth contribute considerably towards sustained burgeoning of the practices directly and indirectly linked to the prevalence of child labour.

**References**

Basu, K. (2003). The Economics of Child Labor. *Scientific American, 289*(4), 84-91.

Basu, K., & Tzannatos, Z. (2003). The Global Child Labor Problem: What Do We Know and What Can We Do? *The World Bank Economic Review, 17*(2), 147-173.

Basu, K., & Van, P. (1998). The Economics of Child Labor. *The American Economic Review, 88*(3), 412-427.

Bhukuth, A. (2008). Defining Child Labour: A Controversial Debate. *Development in Practice, 18*(3), 385-394.

Braun, S. (2006). Core Labour Standards and FDI: Friends or Foes? The Case of Child Labour. *Review of World Economics / Weltwirtschaftliches Archiv, 142*(4), 765-791.

Burra, N. (2001). Cultural Stereotypes and Household Behaviour: Girl Child Labour in India. *Economic and Political Weekly, 36*(5/6), 481-488.

Busse, M., & Braun, S. (2004). Export Structure, FDI and Child Labour. *Journal of Economic Integration, 19*(4), 804-829.

Chandrasekhar, C., & Ghosh, J. (2007). Recent Employment Trends in India and China: An Unfortunate Convergence? *Social Scientist, 35*(3/4), 19-46.

Chowdhury, S. (2011). Employment in India: What Does the Latest Data Show? *Economic and Political Weekly, 46*(32), 23-26.

Das, S., & Mukherjee, D. (2007). Role of women in schooling and child labour decision: the case of urban boys in india. *Social Indicators Research, 82*(3), 463-486.

DC, N., & Wind, S. (2009). Child labour in India: A Nexus among the State, Education and NGO? *The Indian Journal of Political Science, 70*(3), 825-838.

Doepke, M., & Zilibotti, F. (2009). International Labor Standards and the Political Economy of Child-Labor Regulation. *Journal of the European Economic Association, 7*(2/3), 508-518.

Emerson, P., & Knabb, S. (2013). Bounded rationality, expectations, and child labour. *The Canadian Journal of Economics / Revue Canadienne D'Economique, 46*(3), 900-927.

Iversen, V., & Ghorpade, Y. (2011). Misfortune, misfits and what the city gave and took: The stories of South-Indian child labour migrants 1935–2005. *Modern Asian Studies, 45*(5), 1177-1226.

Kovasevic, N. (2007). Child Slavery India's Self-Perpetuating Dilemma. *Harvard International Review, 29*(2), 36-39.

Lieten, G. (2002). Child Labour in India: Disentangling Essence and Solutions. *Economic and Political Weekly, 37*(52), 5190-5195.

Maurya, O. (2001). Child Labour in India. *Indian Journal of Industrial Relations, 36*(4), 492-498.

Mukherjee, D., & Das, S. (2008). Role of Parental Education in Schooling and Child Labour Decision: Urban India in the Last Decade. *Social Indicators Research, 89*(2), 305-322.

Ospina, E., & Roser, M. (2017). Child Labor. *OurWorldInData.org*.

Pande, R. (1996). Elimination of Child Labour: Use or Abuse? *Indian Journal of Industrial Relations, 32*(2), 216-222.

Rao, K., & Rao, M. (1998). Employers' View of Child Labour. *Indian Journal of Industrial Relations, 34*(1), 15-38.

Sumanta, L. (1980). Children without Childhood. *Economic and Political Weekly, 15*(23), 1007-1007.

Togunde, D., & Weber, E. (2007). Parents' views, children's voices: Intergenerational Analysis of Child Labor Persistence in Urban Nigeria. *International Journal of Sociology of the Family, 33*(2), 285-301.

Umapathy, G. (2017). Child Labour in Rural India . *IOSR Journal Of Humanities And Social Science , 22(7)*, 50-52.

Webbink, E., Smits, J., & De Jong, E. (2013). Household and Context Determinants of Child Labor in 221 Districts of 18 Developing Countries. *Social Indicators Research, 110*(2), 819-836.

Weiner, M. (1996). Child Labour in India: Putting Compulsory Primary Education on the Political Agenda. *Economic and Political Weekly, 31*(45/46), 3007-3014.

### 2<sup>nd</sup>. Working women in India

"They destroyed my face, but could not touch my soul" – an excerpt from the memoir of
an acid attack survivor

"I measure the progress of a community by the degree of progress women have achieved"
– Ambedkar

"Social progress can be measured by the social position of the female sex" – Marx

Women in India are the largest structural minority. As a country there has been systemic policy failure which has further oppressed half of the population. This has seriously jeopardized the future of this nation. Further worrisome is the fact that an overwhelming majority of women lack the capability to exercise their agency in a meaningful manner. This creates a situation where women cannot undertake life altering decisions on their own; the Indian society has not been conducive towards the specific needs of women.

The Indian workspace has also not adequately taken cognizance of the societal evils to adequately compensate the working women. This creates hurdles which can often prove to be insurmountable for working women in India. The workspaces in India have to be harmonized to be gender friendly. Although, there can be no one definition of the Indian workspace given the behemoth size of this nation, for the purpose of this paper, an Indian workspace is any place where people come to work to earn their livelihoods. This can range from industries to construction sites. The formal sector has tried to secure certain rights for employed women, but these are often insufficient for larger structural changes. Furthermore, the non-employed women are completely left outside the purview of these measures. As a result the only option left for such women is welfare, which can be extremely problematic. The present notion of welfare wherein certain basic amenities are provided in the form of freebies or doles cannot effectuate liberation for women.

The prevalence of heinous crimes against women like acid attacks, female foeticide, gruesome rapes, and sexual harassment at the workplace create anti-women environments. This further discourages many women from going out to seek gainful employment. The lack of proper support systems for physical and mental health has also proved to be a major impediment for growth and development.

A total of 1.96 crore women quit their jobs between 2004 and 2012 (Andres et al, 2017). The participation of Indian women in the labour force is a mere 27%. This is the lowest amongst the G-20 countries, only better than Saudi Arabia. In comparison, 80% of men participate in the labour force in India.

Global Female Labour Force Participation (%)

| Country | Women in the workforce |
| --- | --- |
| Nepal | 79.9% |
| China | 63.9% |
| Bangladesh | 57.4% |
| United States | 56.3% |
| European Union | 50.8% |
| Sri Lanka | 35.1% |
| India | 27% |
| Pakistan | 24.6% |
| Arab World | 23.3% |

Source: World Bank, 2017.

Examining the women labour force participation rate over time one can conclude that there has been a stark fall in the overall participation rate. This is pertinently counter intuitive.

Women Labour Force Participation (%)

| Year | Participation |
| --- | --- |
| 1990 | 34.80% |
| 1995 | 35.40% |
| 2000 | 33.90% |
| 2005 | 36.90% |
| 2010 | 28.60% |
| 2013 | 27.00% |
| 2016 | 23.70% |

Source: ILO; Government of India – Ministry of Labour and Employment

Over a span of 16 years the women workforce participation rate has decreased by almost 10%. During this corresponding time when ≈2 crore women lost their jobs, 2.43 crore jobs were given to men in India. This is a disturbing trend. Many reasons can be attributed for this phenomenon.    1) Due to greater informalization of women's work they might be falling out of the formal employment channels. This leads to further marginalization and lack of decent and dignified work. 2) Lesser women might be actually working because of lack of work.    3) Due to the rigid family structures and lack of agency for women in India, women from middle and upper classes might find it increasingly difficult to work because their husbands might be earning enough for sustenance of the family. However, this is not true for women from underprivileged communities because of very low salaries both the spouses have to work for sustenance of the family.

Furthermore, there are also no positive linkages between educational attainment and subsequent employment opportunities for women. 67% of girls who graduate in rural India do not work. In urban areas this figure is 68% (UNDP, 2015).

Women who earn are positively predisposed towards better health facilities, increased status in family, and greater avenues to exercise agency within families and socio-economic-cultural structures as compared to those who do not earn. Social, cultural, and economic structures have been historically discriminatory towards women, chief amongst them being patriarchy. In places where there is a prevalence of out-migration of men in search of work, women have an increased share in the labour force. This happens because in the absence of men, women need not "seek permission" to work and hence participate in greater number in the labour force.

A research by Harvard Kennedy School (2016) found that women are under immense constraints of household work and family responsibilities. Women quit their jobs in overwhelming numbers citing "family reasons" as the primary cause. Furthermore, social norms about "appropriate behaviour" significantly limit women's ability to be mobile outside the house, and if one cannot go out then it is impossible to find jobs. Even when women are "allowed" to work, they must make sure that their familial responsibilities and household chores are first taken care of. Also, there are many other requirements which need to be fulfilled like, proximity of the workplace from home, working hours in consonance with the household responsibilities, safe and affordable public transport, and overall safety. The lack of suitable infrastructure like hostels for unmarried single women, crèches for working mothers further accentuates the structural barriers that women need to surmount. Sometimes these obstacles become insurmountable and that is one of the biggest socio-economic concerns of the contemporary milieu.

Since it is legally mandated to have crèches if there are women on the payroll, many employers avoid hiring women. Furthermore, women are also limited to certain occupations, like being beauty and healthcare professionals. These have been considered as traditionally women dominated professions and continue to be so. The sectors which have the highest growth rates and maximum new employment opportunities like telecom, banking, and the core industries are all overwhelmingly dominated by men.

Labour Force Participation in Sectors with Maximum Growth

| Sectors | Men | Women |
|---|---|---|
| Telecom | 84% | 16% |
| Banking and Financial Services | 79% | 11% |
| Core Sectors (Oil, Gas, Steel, Minerals, etc.) | 75% | 25% |

Source: India Skills Report, 2017

Women employees working in the corporate sector in India, especially in the top management profiles generally belong to a very niche socio-economic background. They are found at the intersection of upper class, dominant castes, and mostly urban populace. Women from rural areas and those from predominantly underprivileged backgrounds find it very difficult to enter the corporations in India.

Thus, the existence of insurmountable invisibilized structural barriers cannot be refuted.

There are a few examples of women from underprivileged backgrounds who have made it to the top management schools, and reached the corporate boardrooms, but exceptions cannot be examples. This is because the skills required for being a corporate leader like, fluent English communication skills, top management degree, networks, etc. come from being located in a certain section of the society.

A comprehensive research by McKinsey & Company and LeanIn.Org (2017) studied 132 companies which employ more than 4.6 million people; 34000 employees were also surveyed individually to understand their lived experiences on issues like gender, career opportunities, and work-life balance related issues. In corporations women tend to "fall behind early" and "keep on losing ground at every step" (MKC, 2016; 2015; 2012). Women employees find it difficult for getting the first critical promotion to Manager. This effectively makes it difficult for them to access higher leadership roles. This is one of the reasons why there is a minuscule participation of women in top management roles.

Although most of the companies commit to the principles of gender diversity on paper, in practice it becomes increasingly difficult for women to break the glass ceiling. Women in business are still not considered as a business imperative but rather as something which needs to be forced upon organizations. On average women are hired in less numbers as compared to men. They are also promoted less specially for higher leadership positions. Even at senior roles women are shifted away from "line functions" to "staff functions", thereby rendering women ineligible for chief executive roles.

Thus, in conclusion it is worthwhile to mention that for any country to attain meaningful growth and development it is extremely essential that women are given their due rights, not only as members of society but also as foundations of family units. Till the time the efforts of working women in all its forms and varieties is adequately recognized and represented we can only wait to see meaningful change on the ground.

References

Adams, J. (2007). Stained Glass Makes the Ceiling Visible: Organizational Opposition to Women in Congregational Leadership. *Gender and Society, 21*(1), 80-105.

Andersson-Skog, L. (2007). In the Shadow of the Swedish Welfare State: Women and the Service Sector. *The Business History Review, 81*(3), 451-470.

Bafana Khumalo. (2005). The Role of Men in the Struggle for Gender Equality: Possibilities for Positive Engagement. *Agenda: Empowering Women for Gender Equity,* 88-95.

Beckman, C., & Phillips, D. (2005). Interorganizational Determinants of Promotion: Client Leadership and the Attainment of Women Attorneys. *American Sociological Review, 70*(4), 678-701.

Berrebi, C., Martorell, F., & Tanner, J. (2009). Qatar's Labor Markets at a Crucial Crossroad. *Middle East Journal, 63*(3), 421-442.

Bertrand, M., Goldin, C., & Katz, L. (2010). Dynamics of the Gender Gap for Young Professionals in the Financial and Corporate Sectors. *American Economic Journal: Applied Economics, 2*(3), 228-255.

BEVELANDER, D., & PAGE, M. (2011). Ms. Trust: Gender, Networks and Trust—Implications for Management and Education. *Academy of Management Learning & Education, 10*(4), 623-642.

Bilchitz, D. (2010). Do Corporations Have Positive Fundamental Rights Obligations? *Theoria: A Journal of Social and Political Theory, 57*(125), 1-35.

Bilimoria, D. (2006). The Relationship Between Women Corporate Directors and Women Corporate Officers. *Journal of Managerial Issues, 18*(1), 47-61.

Blackmore, J. (2015). Disciplining Academic Women: Gender Restructuring and the Labour of Research in Entrepreneurial Universities. In Thornton M. (Ed.), *Through A Glass Darkly: The Social Sciences Look at the Neoliberal University* (pp. 179-194). ANU Press.

Bolino, M. (2007). Expatriate Assignments and Intra-Organizational Career Success: Implications for Individuals and Organizations. *Journal of International Business Studies, 38*(5), 819-835.

Bolton, S., & Muzio, D. (2008). The paradoxical processes of feminization in the professions: The case of established, aspiring and semi-professions. *Work, Employment & Society, 22*(2), 281-299.

Campbell, J. (2007). Why Would Corporations Behave in Socially Responsible Ways? An Institutional Theory of Corporate Social Responsibility. *The Academy of Management Review, 32*(3), 946-967.

Carrim, N. (2016). Gender and Cultural Identity Work of Unmarried Indian Breadwinner Daughters in South Africa. *Journal of Comparative Family Studies, 47*(4), 441-462.

Coleman, I. (2010). The Global Glass Ceiling: Why Empowering Women Is Good for Business. *Foreign Affairs, 89*(3), 13-20.

Coleman, S., & Robb, A. (2009). A Comparison of New Firm Financing by Gender: Evidence from the Kauffman Firm Survey Data. *Small Business Economics, 33*(4), 397-411.

Cragg, W. (2012). Ethics, Enlightened Self-Interest, and the Corporate Responsibility to Respect Human Rights: A Critical Look at the Justificatory Foundations of the UN Framework. *Business Ethics Quarterly, 22*(1), 9-36.

Crane, A., & Matten, D. (2008). Incorporating the Corporation in Citizenship: A Response to Néron and Norman. *Business Ethics Quarterly, 18*(1), 27-33.

Crowley, M. (2013). Gender, the Labor Process and Dignity at Work. *Social Forces, 91*(4), 1209-1238.

Dencker, J. (2008). Corporate Restructuring and Sex Differences in Managerial Promotion. *American Sociological Review, 73*(3), 455-476.

Di Cori, P. (2007). Comparing Different Generations of Feminists: Precariousness versus Corporations? *Feminist Review,* (87), 136-140.

DRIES, N., PEPERMANS, R., HOFMANS, J., & RYPENS, L. (2009). Development and validation of an objective intra-organizational career success measure for managers. *Journal of Organizational Behavior, 30*(4), 543-560.

Dubuc, C. (2012). When Women Are in Charge: The Language Japanese Women Speak at Work. *Anthropologica, 54*(2), 293-308.

# <u>Index</u>

**List of abbreviations**

## List of abbreviations

| | |
|---|---|
| AIBEA | All India Bank Employees Association |
| AIBOC | All India Bank Officers' Confederation () |
| ATM | Automated Teller Machine |
| BMB | Bharatiya Mahila Bank |
| BOB | Bank of Baroda |
| CBS | Core Banking Systems |
| CMD | Chairman & Managing Director |
| CRISIL | Credit Rating Information Services of India Limited |
| ED | Executive Director |
| FinTech | Financial Technology |
| GM | General Manager |
| HDFC | Housing Development and Finance Corporation |
| IBPS PO | Institute of Banking Personnel Selection Probationary Officer |
| ICICI | Industrial Credit and Investment Corporation of India |
| IT | Information Technology |
| NOBW | National Organization of Bank Workers |
| NPA | Non-Performing Assets |
| PNB | Punjab National Bank |
| PSB | Public Sector Bank |
| PSU | Public Sector Undertaking |
| RBI | Reserve Bank of India |
| SBI | State Bank of India |
| UFBU | United Forum of Bank Unions |
| USA | United States of America |

<u>**Introduction:**</u>

The principal objective of setting up banks in most countries of the world was to mobilize savings and apportioning them for productive uses (Bagchi & Banerjee, 2005). One of the earliest analyses of savings and industry was made by David Hume in his 1752 classic "Of Money". The banking sector in India has undergone tremendous growth since independence. As per the RBI data total deposits in the banks grew from Rs. 6000 crores in 1970-71 to Rs. 15,00,000 crores in 2003-04; the outstanding credit in the respective years stood at Rs.5000 crore and Rs. 8,40,000 crores (PWC, 2010).

The Narasimhan Committee (1998) recommended consolidation of banks and the formation of 3-4 large banks with global coverage (Sahoo, 2017). P. Chidambaram in 2008-09, as the then Finance Minister mooted the same issue. Arun Jaitley (Finance Minister, 2017) and Urjit Patel (RBI Governor, 2017) took this idea further and consolidated SBI and its associate banks (Anand, 2017).

It was predicted that when State Bank of India (SBI) would be merged with all its subsidiaries, the new agglomerated entity would be among the top 10 banks in the world (PWC, 2010; The Hindu, 2012). But, the outcome was rather dismaying. Even the new consolidated SBI could just reach the top 50 global banks, unlike the prophesied top 10 (Sharma, 2017).

This paper will explore the envisaged plan of "banks consolidation" and its impacts on the employees of these banks. The paper has been divided into four sections: introduction, pros, cons for labour per se, and conclusion. The pros and cons would include a comparative analysis of both the benefits and drawbacks of the consolidation move, and its impacts on the employees of these banks. This paper is the culmination of an earlier presentation. Thus, the scope of the paper would be limited thenceforth. The main objective of this paper would be to delve into certain critical viewpoints in this whole episode of bank consolidation, and to raise analytical questions with respect to the future positioning of labour in the banking sector.

Some of the popular arguments for consolidation of banks include India's need for large banks with global reach, so as to be capable of financing giant infrastructure projects (Ralli, 2017). However, the neo-liberal policies and hope for the trickle-down effect of these giant financiers to reach the poorer strata of the society has been proved fallible repeatedly.

The issues of the Non-Performing Assets (NPAs) of these banks would be problematic to deal with. The capital ratio of 16 of the 21 Public Sector Undertakings (PSU) banks is close to the regulatory minimum, with the possibility of breaching it (Sharma, 2017). The Indian government started the recent process of bank consolidation with the country's biggest lender, the SBI, in which government has a 61.23% stake (Sahoo, 2017). On 23$^{rd}$ August 2017, the Union Cabinet of India had given an in-principle approval towards the merger of PSU banks like Bank of Baroda (BoB), Punjab National Bank (PNB) (Ohri, 2017). This paved the way for the government's ambitious neo-liberal plan for consolidation among state-run lenders. This was purportedly to help them gain efficiency and to reap the benefits of scale. Following the spread of this news the share prices of the respective banks followed an upward trajectory (Surabhi, 2017). But do these surges imply any benefits for the employees? Is the "free market" really worried about the thousands of employees in the banking sector? With the rapid loss of jobs in this sector and incessant casualization the fate of labour in Indian banking and financial systems is undergoing a paradigm shift, albeit adversely deleterious to labour.

The governments, permeating the party lines, have been continuously adamant about the creation of six large public sector banks operating at global scale to put India on the world map (Dangwal, 2017).

### Pros:

Despite the fears due to the financial crisis in the USA and Europe that proved the hypothesis that "big banks cannot fail" erroneous, there does exist some advantages for having large banks (Pradeep, 2012). Bigger banks can better utilize the efficiencies of scale. The scarce talent in terms of human resources for particular banking related services could be better used than in a smaller bank. There would also be a possibility for better usage of the brand equity and capital utility optimization. Most of the pro-consolidation economists opine that larger the balance sheet one is working on, more is the ability to weather economic hardships (Poovanna, 2016).

According to many analysts the mergers and consolidation of banks will help in faster resolution of the bad loans in the Public Sector Banks (PSBs) (Dangwal, 2017). Krishnan Sitaraman, Senior Director of CRISIL Ratings, a financial advisory firm, was of the view that PSBs will benefit tremendously from operational and functional synergies in case of a consolidation. This would also result in effective resolution of non-performing assets across lenders (Shukla & Rangan, 2017).

It must also be noted that the current challenges faced by PSBs are far more critical than a merger. It is a struggle for survival for PSBs with the advent of digital banking initiatives by the private banks and FinTech companies at a rapid pace, PSBs are facing huge competition and may stand to lose market share (Saha, 2016).

Earlier one of the barriers to bank consolidation was the varied information technology (IT) platforms and their different interfaces used by banks.  But, now it is a non-issue. Most of the banks are now operationally integrated with Core Banking Solutions (CBS). Almost all of these platforms are capable of communicating with each other. Similar is the case with ATMs. Consolidation also stands to improve the professional standards of the banks. Many posts like CMD, ED, GM, and Zonal Managers will be abolished; this would result in crores of worth of savings for the banks (Anand, 2017).

### SBI Consolidation:

On 1$^{st}$ April 2017, five associate banks and the Bharatiya Mahila Bank (BMB) became a part of the SBI. This propelled the largest lender of India into the list of top 50 banks worldwide. Bank of Saurasthra was merged with SBI in 2008, and State Bank of Indore in 2010. The merged entity now has a total employee base of around 2,77,270, the highest in the country (Jain, 2016). The second highest is HDFC bank at 76,286. The merged entity also has a deposit base close to Rs. 26 Lakh crores, which is almost double the budget of India (Rs. 14 lakh crores) (Sharma, 2017). Thus, what merits our attention is the behemoth that has been created by this merger.

### Cons:

The present SBI chief Arundhati Bhattarcharya had previously gone on record saying that "the merger is not a priority at the current juncture" (Saha, 2016). Then why was there a sudden change of heart after the consolidation? Was it government pressure? Vested interests and lobbying to satiate industrial greed? Or just poor policy vision?

Never once is the opinion of the employees of the banks taken into consideration. The real issue that should haunt the PSBs is Non-Performing Assets (NPAs). The recovery of bad loans should be the highest on the agenda since the total NPAs in Indian banks is now close to Rs. 7 lakh crores (Dangwal, 2017). In such a situation will the idea of consolidation of banks truly resolve the problem of NPAs?

Or is this just a clever way to divert the attention away from the recovery of loans crisis? Like the whole episode on demonetization and black money. Demonetization was claimed to be a "master stroke" to eradicate black money. However, it has absolutely not served the requisite economic purposes.

Despite the RBI repeatedly announcing numerous restructuring schemes, the bad loans have been continuously rising. From Rs. 2,61,843 crores to Rs. 7,00,000 crore at present. This is a rise of more than 200% in about two years (Sahoo, 2017). This is particularly worrying. RBI's financial stability report had also warned about the gross bad loan ratio of the system rising to 10.2% in March 2018 from 9.6% in March 2017 (Surabhi, 2017).

In strong opposition to the consolidation move a nation-wide strike was carried out by the employees of the PSBs. They protested against this move. This strike was carried out under the aegis of United Forum of Bank Unions (UFBU). The UFBU brings together nine different unions, including the All India Bank Officers' Confederation (AIBOC), the All India Bank Employees Association (AIBEA), and the National Organization of Bank Workers (NOBW) (Ralli, 2017). This shows that the officers, employees, and workers are all unanimous in their opposition to the proposal.

AIBEA General Secretary CH Venkatachalam said, "Government talks only about consolidation, merger, and amalgamation of banks, whereas in reality, India needs more banking services".

Bank mergers would also result in the closure of many bank branches, as is already happening in the case of SBI. Big banks would also increase the risk for these large lenders, since the risks will start getting concentrated in single balance sheets without diversification. The consolidation of banks will result in the reduction of close to 50% of jobs in the PSBs. The trend has already started, this year the vacancies for IBPS PO have been reduced drastically with seven banks announcing zero vacancies, including the Bank of Baroda, which is one amongst the largest banks in India (Ohri, 2017). In a country like India can we afford this when unemployment is one of the most serious concerns of the contemporary political economy? The demographic dividend if not utilized will soon turn into demographic disasters. In such circumstance how can the government justify cutting down on thousands of well-paying jobs?

The UFBU, which claims a membership base of nearly 10 lakh employees across banks intensely opposed this consolidation move and raised the various concerns. They also asked the government for cost reimbursement for slogging numerous extra hours during demonetization. On 22nd August 2017, 21 public sector banks' employees, controlling close to 75% of the total banking business in India, went on strike. However, operations at private lenders such as ICICI Bank, HDFC Bank, Axis Bank and Kotak Mahindra Bank were normal (Surabhi, 2017). Never do the employees of private sector banks ever go on strike. This shows that the employees in private sector banks do not even have the freedom to go on strikes, unlike their government serving counterparts. On 15th September 2017 there is also a massive rally which has been planned by the UFBU.

But the bigger question here is, whether the opposition by banking unions ever taken into consideration? Are the employees every heard? If we go by the retrospective examples the answer seems to be glaringly nugatory. The employees are never heard when it comes to macro scale policy decisions. On 4th June 2015 more than 50,000 employees of the associate banks of SBI called for a strike and did not work to register their fervent protest against the merger with SBI (Das, 2015). Nevertheless, the merger was subsequently carried out without paying any heed to the opinions of the employees.

## Conclusion:

The banking sector in India directly employs over 13 lakh people, including both public and private sector banks (Ralli, 2017). But never once is their opinion taken into consideration for any major macro level policy decisions. The PSB employees at the very least call for strikes and get their voice heard in the media, but the private bank employees do not even possess that authority (Balyan, 2011). The increasing contractualization and casualization of labour in both the sectors is a really worrying trend. The voices of the employees are being further stifled by privatization and devolution in government banks.

The popular argument given for bank consolidation is utilization of economies of scale. But for an advanced and risk entailing sector this argument often proves to be fallacious and farcical (Bagchi & Banerjee, 2005). It often proves to be a façade to move the attention from larger failures in the financial management systems and economic conundrums. The move of consolidation, although on paper looks promising and revolutionizing, it is negatively detrimental on labour and also compromises on the entire sustainability of the banking and economic system.

## References:

Bagchi, A., & Banerjee, S. (2005). How Strong Are the Arguments for Bank Mergers? *Economic and Political Weekly, 40*(12), 1181-1189.

Dangwal, S. (2017). PSBs likely to go down from 21 to 12. *India Today*.

Das, S. (2015). SBI associate merger proposal irks employee's unions, strikes to follow. *The Economic Times*.

Jain, M. (2011). Analytical study of labour productivity and its impact on banking sector. *Saurashtra University*.

Ohri, N. (2017). Four large public sector lenders asked to consider mergers. *Bloomberg Quint*.

Poovanna, S. (2016). Do we need consolidation in Indian banking sector. *Live Mint*.

Pradeep, R. (2017). Public Sector Banks consolidate now. *The Hindu*.

PWC. (2010). Cabinet clears alternative mechanism to oversee PSU banks mergers. *The Hindu*.

Ralli, D. (2017). India does not need too many government banks. *Business Standard*.

Saha, M. (2016). Public Sector Banks consolidation: a painful journey. *The Hindu*.

Sahoo, M. (2017). Bigger and stronger is the new motto. *Quartz India*.

Sharma, S. (2017). Number of PSU banks to fall to 10-15: Sanjeev Sanyal. *Live Mint*.

Shukla, S & Rangan, G. (2017). Why the time may be ripe for consolidation. *Economic Times*.

Talwar, S. P. (2001). Competition, consolidation and systemic stability in the Indian banking industry. *BIS Research Paper*.

<u>**4<sup>th</sup>. Underdevelopment – Syria**</u>

"No human is free here" – a Syrian resident citizen living near sniper alleys

Aleppo, Homs, Damascus, cities ravaged by savagery. That is Syria today. External aggression and violence supporting patronage has resulted in one of the greatest world tragedies of our times. Humans have been killed, maimed, and brutalized to a level of human genocide. Syrian citizens who sought refuge elsewhere are also not being allowed to come back to their own country.

Mass protests were responded with violence and terror by the Syrian government. Shrapnels have pierced baby skulls in this country. People are just asking one question, "Where do we go, this is where we live".

The intra-populational ability and capacity to move out of the country in search of safe places also has to be examined. House Assad has brutally controlled and savagely repressed all kinds of opposition in the 40 years of their fiefdom. The media stranglehold is scary and infringing on the most basic rights of freedom. The citizenry has been reduced to rights-less people, pleading for their existence. The right to live for themselves and their families, the situation in Syria is hard to be described through words on paper.

The elites are still able to live and occasionally enjoy their lives (HBO, 2018). A middle class family moving into their semi-destroyed house had this to say when asked about their house being bombed again, "Inshallah! Nothing happens". When asked about the government's role in their lives being ravaged, they reply, "The government has no role to play in this". At this very moment the tragedy becomes so clear.

The amount of sadness, grief, loss, and helplessness on the faces of the people was traumatic; their inability to stand up against Assad and the Syrian establishment is a failure of the world order. The "great" nations have not been able to secure justice for the Syrian people. Instead Syria has become a world stage for power projection and blood politics.

No human should have to face this in their lives.

World systems theory – the global capitalism and markets do have an impact on Syria. However, like world empires certain areas of Syria are far more developed and act as "core" turning other areas into "peripheries". This has led to unending exploitation and loss of human lives. These core areas are also places which are in close proximity to the political and military prowess in Syria. The head of the government has unquestioned power in these areas with psycho-fanatic following.

Structuralism – since the industrial and other sectors of the Syrian economy have been severely impaired the prospects for its people. Employment is another serious concern for the youth. Many of the radicalized youth have taken up arms so that they can avail of some monetary benefits.

Dependency Theory – the existence of metropolises and satellites is true in Syria. The metropolises may also become satellites in due course. Certain cities in Syria have been able to maintain their lives at the cost of other regions in the country. Historical processes have also led to underdevelopment in Syria. The ethnic tensions, historical power obsession, brutal state repression, etc. have accentuated Syria's underdevelopment.

Imperialism and its developmental implications – although the contemporary Syrian republic's genesis can be traced to Islamic and French imperialism, the consequential effects of colonialism cannot be clearly identified right now. Due to the violence existing in the country from 2011 the people have been seriously battered not by some external imperialist but by various home grown fanatics and arms wielding state apparatus. All armed sides have contributed equally to the underdevelopment of Syria and worsening the life conditions of its people. The Kurdish population has been disenfranchised and violated at multiple levels.

Theory of unequal exchange – this theory of underdevelopment holds true for Syria. The wages in Syria are paltry. Even when the Syrian refugees travelling to developed parts of the world, their labour will never be at par with the original inhabitants of the country they are seeking refuge in. As a result they have to work for less than equal wages. Capital investments in the country have also not been adequate to improve the lives of people and the conditions of the country.

Circular causation, backwash, and spread effect – circular causation has had the most severe and brutal consequences in Syria. The negatives have continuously added up to create a negative atmosphere for the people. The positives have been non-existent in Syria.

Neo-liberal arguments of international integration – global production systems, offshoring, and value chains, new trade regimes (Paul, 2018) – the idea that free world trade will integrate the world economy has proved to be an utter failure for Syria. The country has been brutalized and ravaged by various external agents. The economic growth of the country has therefore severely and irreparably suffered. The concept of a free market eventually helping the people in a country to lead better lives has also not been successful in Syria. The nature of the existing market in the country is open to debate and deliberations.

References

Paul, B. (2018). Theories of Underdevelopment and Unequal Exchange. *SMLS, TISS*.

HBO. (2018). This is what life is lie inside Assad's Syria. *Vice*.

# 5<sup>th</sup>. Consumption in India – 1950 – 2014

Private consumption in India accounted for 57.8% of the nominal GDP in March 2018 (CEIC, 2018). The corresponding figure in the previous quarter was 62.2%. From 1996 to 2018 the average share of private consumption has been 59.1%.

Consumption patterns in rural India are outpacing urban consumption; this positive change is happening because of good rainfall and increased government spending on infrastructure (Agarwal, 2018). However, the living conditions in rural India are still far below acceptable global human living standards. This is of concern for a country with overwhelming populations living and surviving in the hinterlands. As cities start reaching their saturation points it is important that meaningful economic avenues for livelihood generation are created close to places where people live. Migrant workers have to face a plethora of challenges and attacks on their human dignity when they are forced to work for pittances.

Furthermore, the Indian populace spends a large portion of their income on living essentials. The reasons for this can be attributed to meagre income levels, family sizes, single earning members, lack of institutional support, etc. The workers in the informal sector are at accentuated vulnerabilities because their survival can depend on their ability to work and earn for the day. These vulnerable workers have to undergo severe strains on their health to be able to consume and feed themselves and their families. The aspirations for a decent life are often non-existent or extremely vague and far-fetched in the popular imagination of vulnerable populaces.

The intra-populational disparities in consumption can often portray different story. However, this does not lead to the betterment of the consumption patterns of say, an entire village. For larger structural changes it is important to have meaningful policy decisions in that direction. For instance workers are still paid meagre wages in the range of six thousand to ten thousand rupees in metropolitan cities of India. The level of exploitation in the informal sector is horrifying. The entry level wages in formal sector organizations is also very low for consuming and surviving decently. Nevertheless, there is a scope for career development and enhancement in the formal sector which is completely absent in the informal sector. Workers are struck in a quagmire with no possibility for respite. This is extremely worrisome.

Healthy consumption levels can often induce positive changes in the society. Thus, it is of pertinent importance that people have the ability to earn and consume to lead a meaningful life.

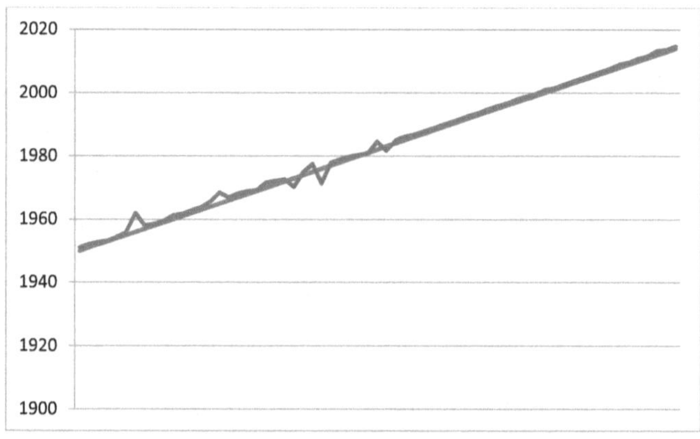

Trend Line for Consumption from 1950 – 2014

(Data – Penn World Tables)

Consumption is calculated by computing both private and government consumption for the country. Output GDP is computed at constant prices.

Marginal Propensity to Consume = (C2 – C1)/(Y2-Y1)

C1 and C2 are consumption levels, and Y1 and Y2 are income levels.

| Consumption | GDP (Output) | Year | MPC |
| --- | --- | --- | --- |
| 310180.0625 | 315490.5938 | 1950 | 1.012254078 |
| 322501.1875 | 327662.5625 | 1951 | 1.110397496 |
| 332102.0313 | 336308.875 | 1952 | 0.809298124 |
| 347555.7813 | 355404.125 | 1953 | 0.268072612 |
| 351547.1563 | 370293.2813 | 1954 | 0.25416659 |
| 353268.5313 | 377065.9063 | 1955 | 0.880935039 |
| 366535 | 392125.4375 | 1956 | 5.95142009 |
| 371171.1563 | 392904.4375 | 1957 | 1.019368461 |
| 397798.8125 | 419026.1563 | 1958 | 0.4808894 |
| 400047.4063 | 423702.0625 | 1959 | 0.578411963 |
| 421776.5 | 461268.875 | 1960 | 1.239772924 |
| 441677.2188 | 477320.7813 | 1961 | 0.726676027 |
| 456540.2188 | 497774.1875 | 1962 | 0.821496067 |
| 482729.7188 | 529654.4375 | 1963 | 0.853877568 |
| 514811.5 | 567226.3125 | 1964 | 1.5966353 |
| 501068.0625 | 558618.5625 | 1965 | 3.453422053 |
| 499932.75 | 558289.8125 | 1966 | 1.057761004 |
| 548087.1875 | 603814.6875 | 1967 | 1.157515238 |
| 580645.125 | 631942.125 | 1968 | 0.921072587 |
| 639707.0625 | 696065.125 | 1969 | 0.206872488 |
| 641948.875 | 706901.8125 | 1970 | 1.556949365 |
| 680184.4375 | 731459.8125 | 1971 | 1.204453713 |
| 698665.5 | 746803.75 | 1972 | 0.580539199 |
| 723805.75 | 790108.75 | 1973 | -2.700091489 |
| 736348.6875 | 785463.375 | 1974 | 0.857460369 |
| 807913.5625 | 868924.8125 | 1975 | 2.539801294 |
| 770910.5625 | 854355.5625 | 1976 | -4.609169878 |
| 766499.875 | 855312.5 | 1977 | 0.723219316 |
| 758798.3125 | 844663.5 | 1978 | 0.967232092 |
| 706734.6875 | 790836.0625 | 1979 | 0.767067132 |
| 723271.3125 | 812394.3125 | 1980 | 0.372885594 |
| 721407.1875 | 807395.125 | 1981 | -0.223609355 |
| 723529.6875 | 797903.125 | 1982 | 2.57882834 |
| 741346.8125 | 804812.125 | 1983 | -1.298229372 |
| 744151.3125 | 802651.875 | 1984 | 0.889016987 |
| 759573.8125 | 819999.6875 | 1985 | 1.050741119 |
| 811690.375 | 869599.5 | 1986 | 0.718048014 |
| 852100.1875 | 925876.8125 | 1987 | 0.691175914 |
| 906872.25 | 1005121.563 | 1988 | 0.672477043 |
| 956308.9375 | 1078635.875 | 1989 | 0.694340063 |
| 1009432.375 | 1155145.125 | 1990 | 0.58081585 |
| 1021609.688 | 1176111 | 1991 | 0.560618172 |
| 1063515.125 | 1250859.625 | 1992 | 0.65753932 |
| 1118335 | 1334230.875 | 1993 | 0.592731998 |

| | | | |
|---|---|---|---|
| 1173018.75 | 1426488 | 1994 | 0.798898452 |
| 1261281.75 | 1536968.875 | 1995 | 0.788762747 |
| 1364542.625 | 1667883.875 | 1996 | 0.6226616 |
| 1426601.75 | 1767551.375 | 1997 | 0.885347589 |
| 1538181 | 1893580.125 | 1998 | 0.880439865 |
| 1661990.875 | 2034202.875 | 1999 | 0.551414009 |
| 1718396.875 | 2136496.25 | 2000 | 0.906122034 |
| 1823006.625 | 2251944 | 2001 | 0.355902856 |
| 1872235.375 | 2390264.75 | 2002 | 0.504240599 |
| 1989047.5 | 2621924.25 | 2003 | 0.543712595 |
| 2102790 | 2831120.25 | 2004 | 0.609858678 |
| 2348680.75 | 3234313.25 | 2005 | 0.547219332 |
| 2547221.5 | 3597130.75 | 2006 | 0.692378502 |
| 2826269.25 | 4000158.5 | 2007 | 0.634824869 |
| 3115732.25 | 4456131.5 | 2008 | 1.041483324 |
| 3413841.75 | 4742367 | 2009 | 0.533887504 |
| 3770315.5 | 5410061.5 | 2010 | 0.773593211 |
| 4186397.25 | 5947917.5 | 2011 | 0.589773528 |
| 4396150.5 | 6303568 | 2012 | 1.288629411 |
| 4683861.5 | 6526837 | 2013 | 0.684663671 |
| 4991770.5 | 6976560 | 2014 | 0.715505994 |

References

CEIC. (2018). India Private Consumption.

Agarwal, S. (2018). India's rural consumption surges in boost for FMCG firms. *Livemint*.

## The Sabha

- against inequality

*The trails to traverse,*

*the paths to find,*

*the journeys to experience,*

*the emotions to feel.*

*Some, with elation and delight,*

*others, bewitching blinding nights.*

-Swarnava

# Index

Image List

| Picture 1 | Organization Structure Chart |
|-----------|------------------------------|
| Picture 2 | Rains & Choking Spaces – the daily wage earner |
| Picture 3 | Young and Aspiring |

"Go, take our voice to everyone. There are no politicians or media for the poor" – a woman whose home (shanty) was demolished.

"Poverty is the worst form of violence" – Gandhi

"From each according to his ability to each according to his need" – Marx

## 1. Introduction

The Sabha endeavours to provide digital and print media which is accessible and reader friendly. The present corporate media can often neglect the needs of various marginalized sections of our society due to a plethora of reasons and vested interests. The Sabha seeks to provide a platform where people from all intersections of structural oppression can write, contribute, and be heard.

The Sabha has covered stories where there was no accessibility to the conventional media. These places are perhaps extremely remote to garner any popular media attention. Some of such places are Gram Sabha elections in Jharkhand, Remote North Eastern regions, tribal regions in M.P,

These stories were extremely important for the Indian populace; these not only bring out the inherent failures of the structural systems but also set a narrative to secure the rights of the most impoverished. For instance, a senior citizen woman in rural area after getting government rehabilitation could only build a "*kaccha*" house for herself, with no basic amenities like water, sanitation, electricity, etc. She also had to sell her livestock of 3 goats to be able to build even that. The feeling of helplessness that was brought out to the people through the digital mediums of The Sabha brought out the realities that exist in these neglected areas.

The farmers asking difficult questions like is giving up agricultural land for various "schemes" and accepting "compensation" in the form of land or money sustainable in the long run? This is something which raises questions which are important not only for the policy makers but also for the average citizen.

The stories about Women Trade Union leaders complaining about the lack of women leadership in Trade Unions is a serious matter of concern for the entire labour movement and the workforce. In women labour intensive industries like garment manufacturing, when an entire project is closed because a sexual harassment case has been filed by a worker against a supervisor, what the entire country needs to ask is how a company can so easily violently thwart the basic rights of the workers without any moral or ethical crisis. These are very important questions that organizations and managements have to answer for themselves and the constitutional republic.

In other stories African-American Women Trade Union Leaders in Boston explain how the intersectionalities of gender, race, and poverty operate to continually disenfranchise communities. They also bring out important discussion points like how it is of paramount importance that they continue to have the leadership which is from amongst them. The networks that are being built with women construction workers in India were also highlighted.

Stories like the Bodo-Santhal conflicts in Kokrajhar area near Indo-Bhutanese border are some instances which truly resonate with the organizational ethos of geographical equity.

## 2.  About the Organization

"All theories are provisional, in the sense that it is only a hypothesis, we can never prove it. No matter how many times the results of experiments agree with some theory, we can never be sure that the next time the result will not contradict the theory." – Hawking

Like theories it is also important to question the inherent malaise of various normativities in society. These systemized oppression leads to the people becoming disempowered through various means. The Sabha is a journey which tries to encapsulate these structural injustices being perpetrated on the citizenry and beyond.

The name of the organization "The Sabha" has been conceived and derived from the Hindi word "*Sabha*" meaning congregation; a coming together of ideas, opinions, and aspirations of the various historically and structurally marginalized socio-cultural communities to assert their voices in the politico-economic developments of the country.

This is a digital and print media organization in Mumbai which aims to connect geographies through narratives of University Students, Proles, and Travelers.

The organization is an attempt to build a responsible, peaceful and thinking society. It seeks to make visible the stark inequality that exists at the intersection of multiple layers in our society. We want to interrogate "human nature" and its relationship with the environment, without making anything above questionability in particular.

The content of the narratives intends to be in spatially equitable form. The narratives are also seen with the eyes of social movement and governance in different location, drawing similarity and their difference.

The Sabha also intends to highlight neo-producers in the dominant consumptive society of our times.

The Sabha is a fairly new organization in the media domain, started a few years ago (December, 2014). Presently its operations are funded by Mudra finance schemes, newspaper sales, and subscriptions. No advertisements are taken, which is a unique feat for any media organization.

The organization offers a geographical narrative through print and digital media. The aim is to highlight the political nature of the everyday as experienced across different domains of inequality, caste, class, gender, ethnicity, race, disability. Where views and opinions are from non-static people in motley "sabha" (meeting of individuals/collectives) of producing, feeling, acting, and thinking; university students, transgenders, workers, farmers, travellers, and artists, and "we" is grammarless.

Crime is the mirror of our society. It helps us to identify what has gone wrong within the fault lines of power, of law and media, state and market, people and citizens. While publishing, the organization continuously tries to link daily struggles to global politics, from particular sexuality to ontological universality in longitudinal sense, where the narratives are linked geographically, to decapitalize the data fed from certain regions and capitalise on the problems it manifests.

The Sabha has always believed that we are people before citizens. The journey of the organization has been unconventional, which changed as the people and environment contributed. Starting with a print edition and then moving to the digital world. Presently the organization is planning to make an inclusive editorial board with three editors; Female, Transgender, and Male. The team also includes various university students who will take the organization forward by maintaining and sustaining the core value systems. The organization also seeks to form long lasting relationships with student unions and faculties across the world to collaborate in content, to diffuse the shared chaos and silence. We need to be present tangibly in physical space as well as in bytes of virtual, however small it may be, to keep on saying the truth in real, including the imagination, in all the forms of communication, we are staying alive.

The Sabha has covered various difficult stories like advertisements in media, denotified tribes like the Kataria community in Latur, slum residents whose houses were demolished, Matang procession where there was no other media, etc. These unheard and unregistered stories are what make India truly a melting pot of humanity. As one of the demolition affected woman rightly said, "There are no politicians or media for the poor"

### 3.  Bringing out the voices – Editorial Policy

The Sabha expects an individual to write on the basis of facts and objective data, but that does not mean that the person will not express emotions with it. The writer can write about their various lived realities. The Sabha always endeavours to have writers with diverse lived realities who can contribute in their unique way by writing.

With the rise of policies with zero socio-economic justice all over the world, there has been a steep rise in inequality at an unprecedented rate. Citizens are not able to cope up with their lives as it is heavily depended on a multitude of complex dynamics like the state power structures, unequal markets, lack of skills and livelihoods, etc. The present digital revolution has also not given any significant representation to these oppressed classes. The technology, innovation, and better living standards are extremely concentrated in urban centres and completely anthropogenic in nature. The margins and the environment have been completely forgotten. The Sabha raises such voices from these margins of socio-cultural-econocide.

From local to global level, The Sabha stands in solidarity with anyone fighting against inequalities. In the era of 24*7 instant news, The Sabha focuses on not just breaking the news, but joining them in the narrative, which can have intersectionalities in different domains. The main focus is not only on opinions but about creating narratives which will help to create an equitable and just society.

The Sabha believes that everything is political and so is everyone. There is no separation between politics and economy, society, or technology. Media is more focused on the region where capital resides, and they miss out other regions in the national coverage. The Sabha brings out these stories in geographical equitable form.

## 4.  Organization Structure

The organization has a lean team of 6 members who work on reportage, subscriptions, videography, etc. The team is headed by the Editor. Fellows and Interns join the team on a periodical basis.

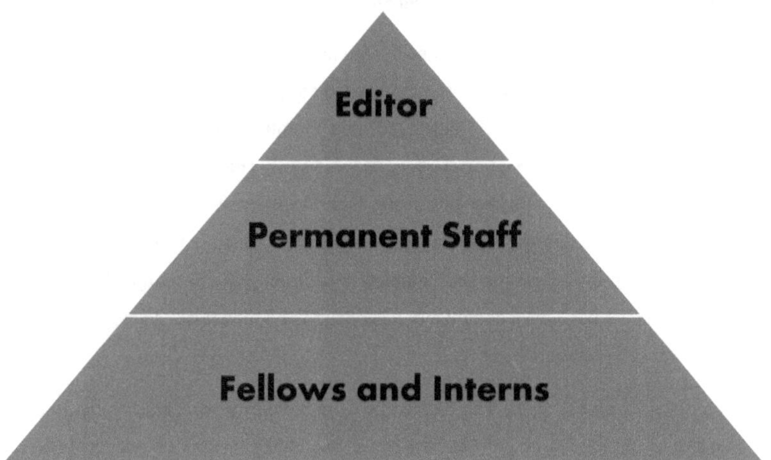

## 5.  The role of Media in a democracy

"Whoever controls the media, controls the mind" – Jim Morrison

"If we don't read the newspaper, we are uninformed; if we read the newspaper, we are misinformed" – Mark Twain

"With great power comes great responsibility" – Voltaire


In any functional democracy media plays a very vital role. Media is often presupposed to act as the fourth pillar of democracy. This ideation is also rooted in the fundamental belief system that media while upholding the democratic principles will also keep in mind the constitutional value systems that need to be further established and emboldened in the country.

However, this is completely absent in the present media regime. We can see the clear rise of a predatorial form of media and news consumption which is critically dependent on showing something as the "other" or "villain". This route of problematization is extremely dangerous for the democratic nation.

Thus, it is of utmost importance for the sub-altern media to capture the popular imagination of the country. This will not only help the citizenry develop a much needed perspective about the socio-economic injustices that have become a structural norm in this nation; and also to develop a sense of conscientiousness as humans.

## 6. The Changing nature of Indian media

Increasingly over the past several years we can see a steep increase in the amount of private media outlets. These organizational changes in the media ownership pattern have exponentially impacted the consumption behaviours. The popular media in various forms like news, movies, digital content shape the behavioural patterns of the populace. This is of extreme cognizance for social psychologists, policy makers, and constitutional bodies.

Thakurta (2012) opines an increasing "corporatization" of the media is to blame for a lot of menace in our society. The absence or increasing decline of not-for-profit media organizations is also a cause of worry (Kumar, 2015; Thakurta, 2012).

### 6.1 Paid News

Paid news is becoming an increasing menace in the media sphere. This is causing severe ramifications in various sections of society, economy, and culture. Such blatant illegalities need to be dealt with at a hastened speed.

There were several instances of paid news in Madhya Pradesh legislative assembly elections. This was brought out to the notice of the Election Commission and the legislator was immediately disqualified (Kaushik, 2017).

However, elections are not the only aspect which paid news indulges in illegalities. There are several other instances where different varieties of venom are spewed on the people consuming such media.

### 6.2 Mobocracy

Venomous media inevitably gives rise to a condition called "mobocracy". There have been several ramifications of this in the past. The killings of rational thinkers, lynching by mobs, student-activist being shot at in the national capital, etc. are instances of mobocracy which have to be taken serious cognizance of by the media organizations and also the policy makers.

### 6.3 Increased Surveillance State

The state through the present regime and bureaucracy has increasingly entered into a surveillance mode wherein the micromanagement of media has become a norm. This is further accentuated when these control networks enter into the editorial spaces of media organizations. Whenever the state has entered into the domain of media there have been gross violations of journalistic ethics.

Also, with increased state surveillance on media there is a strong possibility for the emergence of a post-truth paradigm, which can be extremely dangerous for the society. This can be explained by the rise of fake news phenomenon in our country and different parts of the world, where this phenomenon is further pronounced.

## 7. About the Internship

"Nahi chahieye, aage badho" – a person waiting for the traffic light to go green

This internship gave me some of the most difficult to attain life lesson. The above line was shouted at my face while I was trying to pitch The Sabha fortnightly *patrika* in Mumbai. A man in an uber luxurious vehicle waiting for the traffic light to go green with "Defence" written in bold, capital letter written on his flashy vehicle had this to say when approached with a newspaper. This made me wonder. A lot of interesting thoughts followed, however they are not in the scope of this internship report.

However, what it made me realize is that 93% of the workforce working in the informal sector, have to go through this in uncomfortably quick frequency in their work-lives. Their livelihoods being dependent on their ability to get work, and pay for the most basic necessities make this situation an even difficult predicament. The kind of emotional labour that is exhausted in this process is further worrisome. The life lessons, leadership lessons, and humility that this internship provided me are unparalleled.

Media and journalism are closely interrelated to ethics. Thus, working in the media space one is provided with an opportunity to engage with the ethical paradigms. This internship provided me with such opportunities which allowed me to engage with the various media consumption patterns. The theoretical and social investigation of the contemporaneous trends in media consumption behaviours and the content analysis can be extremely debilitating for an informed citizen.

This internship also provided me opportunities to explore my creative skills for which I am greatly indebted. Having a professional opportunity to develop creative skills can be something which all organizations develop as a culture to foster innovation and thinking abilities.

The internship also forced me to think about the larger solutions to the innumerable challenges faced by the different marginalized communities. It is not just enough to report but also to set a context and appropriate narrative so that the oppressed can get their due share in the shared prosperity of the nation. Otherwise, the entire purpose of nation building can become futile.

# 8. Learning

## 8.1 Organizational Learning

I was introduced to a media organization which truly upholds the spirits of journalism. This is extremely difficult in the contemporaneous milieu of advertisements driven media. But I was fortunate to witness this unique and silent revolution in the media space, both in print and digital. The adequate space for all sections of society is completely absent in the present media consumption patterns, I learnt how organizations wanting to challenge the mainstream can effectively do so by staying true to their organizational culture and value systems.

## 8.2 Ethical Learning

This internship also provided me the opportunities to engage with ethical leadership opportunities. While covering the Mumbai rains, I found impoverished children swimming in the unsanitary rain water on the road, after recording the video, they came up to me and asked me to show it to them. While showing the video to them, I also reminded them to take care of health and hygiene when they swim in the rain waters on the road.

The need of the hour is to not just do our assigned responsibilities but also to go a step further so that the greater good of the world is secured.

## 8.3 Technical Learning

I learned the basics of camera operations and various technical settings related to it. I also learned about how it is important to also capture the context with photos and videos. I used these skills in my photo essays and video essays. While shooting it is also very important to think about the entire team that is involved in the operations and these gave me important team building skills.

I also learned about various digital solutions available in the media and outreach space.

### 8.4 Media and Outreach

I learned how to create outreach programs to take the newspaper to various cross sections of society. I was involved in outreach strategies to increase the visibility for The Sabha in fast moving locations.

As part of the outreach program I was also involved in building relationships with newspaper outlets, academic institutions, libraries, and bulk purchasers; since it is extremely important to look at sustainable sources of revenue and operations management.

I was able to learn a lot about team dynamics, business relationship development, customer outreach, media management, client satisfaction, strategy development, market segmentation, and targeting.

I learned about interviewing techniques used for various interviews.

## 9. Students' Unions in West Bengal

The West Bengal state is facing a unique situation where the students' unions in the state are being completely delegitimized behind the garb of apoliticizing. This is detrimental to the student community in the state. In this regard I did some preliminary research on the subject.

Various students' organizations recently met the education minister in the state assembly. The Mamata Banerjee led state government has vowed to put an end to the democratic student elections and union formation. Partha Chaterjee at the helm of affairs in the state Education Ministry firmly supports this resolve. The state government plans to apply a peculiar model of student councils in place of students unions, wherein the Principal or a Professor will be the President of the student union, and likewise for the post of the Treasurer. This will effectively take away all the executive and financial powers of the union, rendering it completely toothless (SC TH, 2017).

Lyngdoh Committee recommendations like minimum attendance requirements will also be implemented. Quoting the Chief Minister from one of her interviews with a local media channel, "I think holding elections every year is a waste of energy. I will ask the Education Minister to find out whether the St Xavier's model can be adopted." This move is aimed at "depoliticising" the student unions, the proposed changes has intrigued almost the entire student body in the State which has a long history of student politics and produced not only Ministers and MPs, but also Chief Ministers like Buddhadeb Bhattacharjee and Mamata Banerjee herself.

The higher education department on June 7, 2017 issued a notification making student unions apolitical and announcing that polls in colleges and universities would be held every two years. Student elections in West Bengal were last held between December 2016 and January 2017. Colleges and universities have not conducted any elections since the West Bengal College and Universities (Administration and Regulations) Act came into effect.

Student leaders from Jadavpur University opposed this move. Democratic Students Organization demanded greater transparency, online admissions, and eliminating criminals from campuses instead of the government's moves to stifle democratic rights of the students. While all other students unions vehemently resisted this decision, as they thought it would be a direct interference into the democratic rights of the students; Trinamool Chhatra Parishad accepted the proposal of forming the councils. The TMCP claimed that they have always been against the politicisation of education, and want the educational institutions to be free from any political interference. At the same time, they have asked the education minister to "take care" of the posts like general secretary, assistant general secretary, and cultural secretary, so that they should stay in the hands of the students. This in essence is in consonance to the official order passed by the state government.

In between all the politicking the recent harrowing news of a student in a reputed Kolkata college being paraded naked and videographed for questioning the use of students' union funds is something to ponder upon for the entire student body in India (FPS, 2018).

# 10. Mumbai Rains and Choking Spaces

Recently the Kerala Floods tragedy shook the entire nation. The inability of our country to deal with disasters is becoming ubiquitous. This is of grave concern. The urban and rural spaces are equally at stake whenever such conditions arise. Recently while covering the Mumbai rains I could experience first-hand the ability of rains to cripple the city and its people.

The daily wage labourer is particularly hurt whenever such calamities take place because her/his ability to live depends on the day to day earnings which take a critical hit. I met Malamma, a 55 years old daily earner who had very similar things to say.

These children swimming in the rainwater lodged on the roads of Mumbai is a sight which the entire country needs to see. Although, the children might look happy in this photo the concern is far greater.

In urban spaces we constantly see the rise of schooling systems which are extremely unequal in quality and access. The reach of digital content has reached all corners of the society and the aspirations in cities are building. In this context the government infrastructure has systematically failed to solve the urban crisis. The unavailability of access to socio-economically marginalized communities both in rural and urban spaces in widely known.

The complete absence of basic amenities like sanitation and drainage is particularly accentuated in certain pockets of the city. Most of these wards in the city which receive apathy from the state and people have overwhelming majority of oppressed communities living in them. Thus, it comes as no surprise that the entire government machinery works in cahoots with various vested interests to oppress and exploit these communities further.

References

FP Staff. (2018). College student in Kolkata stripped naked, tortured for inquiring about students union expenses. *FirstPost.*

Kaushik, K. What is 'the menace of paid news'?. *The India Express.*

Kumar, S. (2015). Five reasons why media monopolies flourish in India. *Scroll.*

Special Correspondent. (2017). Mamata govt to depoliticise students' unions in Bengal. *The Hindu.*

Thakurta, P. G. (2012). Media Ownership in India-An Overview. *The Hoot.*

*Fighting in the jungles,*

*with brute tentacles.*

*Stomp. Stomp. Stomp.*

*Here comes the state.*

*Criminals!*

*Behind bars.*

*RNI:* **MAHENG/2014/59661**

# P R E S S

## the sabha

**Swarnava S Bhadra**
**Reporter**

*Jun 2018 – Aug 2018*

Owner

**Swarnava S Bhadra**
DOB: 25/08/1995

Annabhau Sathe Nagar,
Mankhurd, Mumbai
www.thesabha.org
swarnava@thesabha.org

The International Labour Organization has developed legal instruments which defines the basic principles and rights at work. These are of two types, conventions and recommendations. Conventions are "legally binding international treaties" which are supposed to be ratified by the member states. Recommendations are "non-binding guidelines". Following the tripartite model, conventions are formulated after consultation and representation from governments, employers, and workers, after which they are adopted at the International Labour Conference (ILO, 2018).

Following this the member states take these conventions to their parliament for ratification. The ILO provides technical assistance if the member states seek so. Complaint procedures can also be initiated against countries if they violate conventions that they have already ratified.

There are eight fundamental core conventions. These conventions have been included as the guiding fundamental principles in close to 1367 ratifications around the globe, covering 91.4% of the total possible number of ratifications. To ensure the objective of universal ratification of all fundamental conventions are achieved, there is a requirement of 129 further ratifications (ILO, 2018).

The eight fundamental conventions are:

1.  Freedom of Association and Protection of the Right to Organize Convention, 1948 (Number 87)
2.  Right to Organise and Collective Bargaining Convention, 1949 (Number 98)
3.  Forced Labour Convention, 1930 (Number 29)
4.  Abolition of Forced Labour Convention, 1957 (Number 105)
5.  Minimum Age Convention, 1973 (Number 138)
6.  Worst Forms of Child Labour Convention, 1999 (Number 182)
7.  Equal Remuneration Convention, 1951 (Number 100)
8.  Discrimination (Employment and Occupation) Convention, 1958 (Number 111)

The democratic republic of India has ratified six of these fundamental ILO Conventions. The two conventions that have not been ratified are Convention Number 87 – Freedom of Association and Protection of the Right to Organize Convention, 1948, and Convention

Number 98 – Right to Organize and Collective Bargaining Convention, 1949. The reasons for the non-ratification of these ILO  Conventions is because of certain restrictions imposed on government employees. According to the Department of Personnel and Training, the ratification of these conventions would mean granting of certain rights that are prohibited under the statutory rules applicable to government servants, like, right to strike for work, openly criticize government policies, freely accept financial contribution, or freely join foreign organizations, etc. To ensure that these statutory laws are taken care of these conventions are not ratified (PIB, 2017).

In India the process of ratification means that the national laws are brought in full consonance and conformity with the provisions of any convention in question. The government also tries to regularly convene tripartite meetings to take various proactive measures.

This paper will look into the conventions related to child labour, its applicability in India. The initiation will be with examining wages within the ambit of decent work.

According to the ILO in the year 1990 there were 79 million "child labour" (Mukherjee & Das, 2008; Bhukuth, 2008; Maurya, 2001) in the world (Basu & Van, 1998); in the year 2013 this figure stood at 265 million (Ospina & Roser, 2017). The child labour force in India has been estimated at around 4.3 million by the 2011 Census, and 10.1 million by UNICEF (Umapathy, 2017). These differences in the total estimation occur because of many reasons including underreporting, and varied technicalities in definitions (Chandrasekhar & Ghosh, 2007).

### Wages and Decent Work

The conventions can be epitomized and espoused in the concept of Decent Work. This section will look into this idea of decent work and how it miserably fails in India.

The various wages that exist and can be defined are: starvation wages, subsistence wages, minimum wages, living wages, and fair wages. This paper will focus on the existence of starvation wages in modern Indian cosmopolitan megacities like Mumbai, Bangalore, Hyderabad, and Delhi. Starvation wages can be defined as wages which cannot satisfy even the most fundamental needs of the worker. This is a modern form of exploitation which is presented behind the garb of employment in various big establishments.

The wages for 12 hours and more of working hours in Indian cities remain to be around Rs. 6000 – Rs. 8000 for establishments like restaurants, shopping complexes including malls, multiplexes, big consumer serving establishments including jewellery shops, etc. This has been found in various recent research studies and reports, also covered by leading national dailies.

The salaries in multinational cloth manufacturing factories still hover around Rs. 7000.

This is an extremely peculiar case of labour exploitation since all these big establishments are registered by the government and are proper tax paying businesses. But, the workers employed in them have no legal rights and function under the broad umbrella of "unorganized workers". Although, they might have legal contracts with their employers, but even those employment contracts specify such salaries blatantly; thus, leaving them with no option for even a legal recourse. This kind of salary structures do not exist in any other modern social democratic states. Thus, it requires introspective, reflective, and critical evaluation as to how India has been able to create such grossly iniquitous structures in the consumerist capitalistic order.

This section will look into these facets of the modern Indian markets.

"Value of labour" is a problematic term. According to Marx (1844), this value is realized only when it is converted into a tangible product, because of the existence of capitalism as the dominant form of political economy. This has become the predicament of the labour. The labourer is no longer the determining agent of his own labour power but the capitalist and the products that is created by the labourer.

This is similar to the value of earth. There cannot be a defined value of earth. It depends on the location and also the resources that need to be exploited. For instance, land in Mumbai is far more expensive than in Jharkhand. But land in and around the gold mines of Jharkhand may be costlier than land in Mumbai. So, the subjectivity of "value" is extremely multidimensional.

Marx (1844) determined that in essence wages are determined through an antagonistic struggle between the capitalist and the worker. Almost always, the capitalist wins. The capitalist or the owner of the means of production can sustain for much longer without the workers, than the workers being able to sustain without them. This is because workers do not possess any of the surplus value that they produce. All of this surplus value is extracted and exploited by the capitalist, thus the worker has to depend on the owners of means of production for their daily sustenance through wages. Also, capitalists have been successful in forming cartels and being cooperative with one another, but this is not true for labour because the relationship between the labouring classes is always competitive. They want to get the work and wages even if it is at the cost of another labour. This is extremely problematic because these strategies have been successful in keeping the overall wages low for the labourers. This also provides the capitalists opportunity to earn even more profits by keeping the market wages low. This can be seen even in contemporaneous Indian milieu.

The capitalist and land owners have various other ways to have a monthly income other than the requisite wages, but the worker does not have any such cushion to fall back on. The labouring class is dependent on its wages to run their homes and feed their families. Thus, they work for whatever wages is offered to them so that they do not die of starvation. This has both metaphorical and literal meaning. Workers at various hierarchies are paid below what their work deserves, at the lower levels the wages are actually starvation wages. But even if we see at the educated skilled levels, like the present case of Indian youth, even they are offered jobs by big corporations which are essentially hand to mouth existence. The capital owners and the land owners can earn interest and rents respectively, but the worker must necessarily toil to earn his wages. This is true even in the present day. This lack of resources amongst workers and the only way of sustenance through wages makes the competition among workers even fiercer.

Thus, the wages given to the working class is just for a "cattle-like existence". Smith (1776) calls this as the "ordinary wage"; this is compatible with the sustenance and reproduction of the labouring race. The demand and supply logic also holds true in case of labour, if the supply of workers far exceeds the demand for it, then a certain section of the labouring class will be condemned into "beggary and starvation". Thus, the worker is completely dependent on the capitalist for their mere survival. This, has changed slightly in the present context, because of the emergence of highly skilled jobs, like, say, computer coding or ethical hacking or neurosciences, the emergence of a highly skilled workforce can sometimes defy this supply demand logic. The demand can at times be more for certain highly skilled jobs. But in general, the capitalists have been successful in keeping the supply always greater than the demand, so that they can always hire at low wage rates and further their profits. This has been the case since the emergence of capitalism.

Also, to keep the prices of commodities close to its natural price it is important to manage the prices of land, labour, and capital, the factors of production. In order to achieve this, almost always the first factor of production which faces the axe is the labour head. This is also true in the present context, innovation, a buzzword of the present milieu has often been synonymous with cost cutting primarily owing to the decreased headcount. Although, it is claimed that innovation and technical advancement leads to the creation of jobs in many other new fields, it is important to examine how this is in accordance to the concept of division of labour. Nobody is against innovation and technological advancement, that is definitely important, but the problem is how do we make it inclusive and accessible to all. How to ensure that innovation is not necessarily synonymous to job loss but to new job creation. The most pertinent understanding which has to be developed is in a consumerist economy it is very important that people have the means to buy what is being produced. The economy does not function only on the thin aired speculations of the stock market, all the hot air results in crashes and economic downturns. This is of special importance in countries like India, with a huge population base of 1.3 billion, we have a ready market, and the only thing required is the purchasing power, which can be attained by giving the fair wages to the workers. Thus, logically putting things into perspective one can very well understand that when workers ask for better wages, it is not really a Marxist revolution, but instead it helps the consumerist capitalistic economy to further, but in a more inclusive and accessible fashion.

That has always been the objective; to provide a minimum decent standard of living for the whole populace. This can be achieved by giving the workers of the world their fair share of wages.

## Worst Forms of Child Labour Convention, 1999 (Number 182) and India

Although India claims that there is a prohibition on child labour in the country, the reality is very different. The rampant use of child labour as the reserve army of cheap labour continues unabated.

The term "child labour" is defined as children between the ages of 5-14 engaged in economic activities and working on a part or full time basis (Doepke & Zilibotti, 2009). Child labour constitutes 13% of the total labour force in India. The total number of child labour has also increased in the urban areas according to the 2001 and 2011 Census reports from 1.3 million to 2 million (Ospina & Roser, 2017). Also, child labour has been increasingly associated with "invisibility". This has happened because of a changing pattern in the location of work from factories to the homes and private spaces of business owners and employers (Basu & Tzannatos, 2003).

Article 24 of the Indian Constitution, which is a fundamental right, prohibits employment of children in factories, mines, and other hazardous industries (Sumanta, 1980), which at present includes mining, explosives, and occupations listed in the Factories Act, 1948. However, employment in non-hazardous industries was not explicitly banned, until recently, and thus provides a lot of scope for exploitation because of the existence of grey areas in the legalities (Lieten, 2002). The Child Labour (Prohibition and Abolition) Act of 1986 was aimed at identifying, prosecuting, and thus putting an end to child labour in India (Basu, 2003).

Child Labour (Prohibition and Prevention) Amendment Act, 2016 puts a complete ban on child labour, below 14 years of age; and bans adolescents, between 14 – 18 years, in hazardous industries (Ministry of Law, GOI).

Poverty is considered to be the primary reason behind children being forced into work (Pande, 1996). In some families the income from children constitute anywhere between 25% - 40% of the total household income (Togunde & Weber, 2007; Rao & Rao, 1998). Lack of resources to attain education has been identified as another major cause behind child labour (Kovasevic, 2007). The Indian government tried to remedy this by introducing the Right to Education Act, a compulsory education policy enshrined as a Fundamental Right in the Constitution. However, even this policy is not able to meaningfully deal with the problem of child labour (DC & Wind, 2009).

Some of the states with the highest number of child labour are Uttar Pradesh (2.1 million), Bihar (1 million), Rajasthan (0.84 million), Madhya Pradesh and Maharashtra (0.7 million each) (Ospina & Roser, 2017). Child labour is also intrinsically linked with various socio, economic, and political circumstances, and vested interests. All these states fall under the classification of "BIMARU" states (except Maharashtra), as coined by Ashish Bose in the mid-1980s, this shows that the education crises in these states have also impacted in high child labour incidences.

A study involving 1535 parents and child labour was conducted by Togunde and Weber (2007). The major cause as identified by them was poverty and the need of future training for careers. Also, an astounding 88.6% of these parents had themselves worked as child labourers while growing up. Thus, there exists a vicious cycle of resource poverty which perpetuates child labour, often intergenerational. 31% of the children believe that their kids would also have to be involved in child labour to enable the financial viability of the household. With the increase in parental education the incidence of child labour decreases drastically. Child labour is more prevalent and gory especially in the less developed nations.

Children are employed, despite legal persecutions, because of the paltry wages they work for. Children work for as low as 1/5th of the amount given to adults. They are also unaware of their rights and hence do not create problems for the employers (Braun, 2006; Rao & Rao, 1998). Child labourers are exposed to a variety of irreversible damages including, but not limited to, physical, psychological, and developmental (Iversen & Ghorpade, 2011). Their overall health, well-being, and growth are stunted (Emerson & Knabb, 2013).

With increasing awareness amongst buyers, international pressures, and advocacy, global corporations have been trying to do away with child labour, at least on paper (Braun, 2006). This leads to greater engagement of child labour in the informal sector and further scope for exploitation. There is a need for consciousness among the corporations to have a child labour free supply chain. The global production networks have to be sanitised for a child labour free production process. Since, in the present conditions, the production processes are extensively outsourced and subcontracted; child labour is still rampantly employed, completely unabated (Busse & Braun, 2004).

Children are employed in a variety of manual works mostly unskilled, domestic labour specially in family owned spaces, agricultural sector, glass industries like bangles, match box making, brass and lock industries, beedi making, rag picking, embroidery, carpet making, fireworks production, mining, quarrying, brick kilns, and tea gardens (Basu, 2003). In urban areas the most widespread is the employment of child labour in the food stalls and restaurants, the quintessential "chotu". Child labour burden is also often gendered. Girls are expected to do most of the domestic and home-based work, which is often unpaid (Burra, 2001). Boys are primarily employed in wage labour outside the house (Das & Mukherjee, 2007).

Directly documenting the experiences of child labour and getting accurate information about their working conditions, wages, timings, etc. proves to be one of the biggest challenges (Kovasevic, 2007). Since almost the entirety of the child labour force is employed in the informal sector it is further difficult to gather reliable information. The children are too scared to talk and the employers are too intimidated by outside interference. In general there is awareness that children must not be employed as workers, but there is also a general fearlessness that nothing concrete is going to happen. A simple lie about the age of the child is enough. Almost any child labour when asked their age would reply "16 or 17 years". Although, 1908, a nation-wide toll free number exists for reporting instances of child labour, the approach is often lackadaisical. Also, the actual child labourers on the field pose a simple question, even to genuinely concerned individuals, "how will we eat and feed our families if we start going to school?" This is a truly confrontational situation.

Since the phenomenon of child labour is multifarious in nature, there is no one way strategy to solve the problem. It requires committed action from various stakeholders, most importantly the government. Bringing financial stability at homes can be one of the entry points to start with the eradication process of child labour. Education is another such entry point (Weiner, 1996). Expanding the educational base, curbing any violence at schools, providing quality, affordable, and universal education can help provide conducive learning, schooling and overall growth environment for children. Vocational training is another mechanism to train the child labourers to have meaningful careers and lives (Maurya, 2001).

Child labour also jeopardizes the future of the children involved by completely ruining the foundational aspects of childhood (Pande, 1996). This has severe repercussions for the society at large, since their chances of becoming positively productive adults diminishes considerably. Countries like India, Pakistan, Bangladesh, and majority of the Sub-Saharan countries are specifically at higher risk. Furthermore, the government educational facilities in all these countries are so abysmal that the chances of any actual upward socio-economic mobility are uncomfortably close to none. Thus, when the parents make a comparative trade-off between the sacrifices required for schooling and the probable benefits, it is a clear choice that they make. Many studies have also elucidated this, as to how many children drop out of school to work because of the inferior quality of education (Mukherjee & Das, 2008). Bourdieu (1986) interestingly initiated the idea of social and cultural capital along with economic capital. Thus, the absence of any of these three can be a contributing factor towards prevalence of child labour in the family.

Basu and Van (1998) have refuted the problematizing of parents as perpetrators of child labour. They have elicited a model in which higher adult wages automatically lead to the extinction of child labour without any bans. However, the empirical evidence for this is missing and it also discounts the fact that many child labourers might not have parents. They might be living with their relatives or foster parents, who most often than not, in the

Indian and less developed countries' context are actually abusive. Therefore, a total ban on child labour might not be the answer, as claimed by Basu and Van, but it can be one of the plausible steps to explore. However, it has to be complemented by various other protection mechanisms like educational and residential facilities for the rescued children.

In a study involving 239120 children spread over 221 districts in 18 developing nations, Webbink, Smits, and Jong (2013) found that 30-50% of children in African countries are involved in child labour, compared to the 4-10% in India and Bangladesh. A comprehensive analysis framework for understanding child labour has been used involving resources, structures, culture, rural vs. urban. The major results they found were that the children were less vulnerable to take up employment if their households were resource sufficient. If the mother is involved in low paying jobs then the children also often participate as non-wage child labour. The family disparities also play a role in this, girls work more than their male siblings; the workload also increases as the size of the family grows.

Iversen and Ghorpade (2011) have studied the work-life histories of 90 individuals who migrated for work before attaining 15 years of age. The period of migration studied is from 1935-2005. Almost all the individuals narrated their experiences of being a child labour before the advent of increased awareness and the lives they had lived. Almost, all of them had to go through extremely gruesome work conditions to afford regular meals. All of them were employed in the lowest paying jobs, and promotions were very rare. Thus, it proved to be an inexorable cycle of never ending poverty and resource scarcity.

If we consider families owning land, the incidence of child labour decreases only after a certain threshold point. The ownership of land is a sign of wealth, especially in rural areas. The land owning pattern can be divided into three categories: marginal, small, and large. The incidences of child labour increases from marginal to small land ownerships; but decreases drastically for large land owning households. In China the child labour participation rate declined from 48% in 1950 to 12% in 1995 (Basu, 2003).

During our field visits to Cheetah Camp, Mankhurd, and Dharavi, we could not overtly see any child labourers working in the manufacturing units. The few children that we did manage to see were too careful about what they revealed to us. Almost, all of them claimed to be "18 years old". All of them denied working in these sweatshops, and claimed that they were only visiting relatives. This illustrates their knowledge about the ban on child labour and the legalities of it. However, this is not true in many of the small food stalls in semi-urban or rural areas. Many shops even in urban areas employ children. Restaurants in Chembur have child labour working as employees, since these are non-hazardous, they even work as waiters. This is particularly worrisome. Nobody would willingly want to become a child labour; this shows a greater malaise in the society. As an envisaged "welfare state", India has not been able to provide economic opportunities for the parents of these adults, neither has it been able to provide appropriate educational and employment opportunities for these youth. The demographic dividend is soon turning into a demographic disaster, which is also visible on the ground. Suddenly in the past few years, a lot of low paying jobs are being taken up by youngsters. This is a visible trend. A lot of middle aged labourers are being replaced with a young labour force. This shows the appalling condition of our employment generation schemes. Almost all of these jobs are extremely low paying, mostly capable of providing only hand-to-mouth existence. Child labourers are paid even lesser.

### Conclusion

This paper has tried to examine two different problems, of child labour and starvation wages.

Starvation wages prove that economic growth and corporate profits are not enough to actually unleash any meaningful development in society unless wages are fair and just. The existence of such dismal starvation wages around the country is also a failure of trickle down economic theories.

There is no easy solution towards eradicating the problems of child labour. The legislations, bans, fundamental rights, all have been tried and all have failed to solve this in its entirety. Thus, there is a need for sustainable global production networks. Confluence between the law and market may be able to provide effective solutions. Millions of childhoods are lost to attain two square meals a day. Close to 8 million children are entrapped in debt bondage, coerced military duty, sexual slavery, etc. These criminalities can be expunged by using a strong law and order machinery. The developed U.S. and E.U. account for almost 0.5 million of these children (Basu, 2003). Trafficking of close to 1.2 million children each year is truly a blot on humanity (Basu, 2003; Webbink et al., 2013). However, problematizing child labour without taking into consideration the extreme economic and social marginalization of these families can turn out to be extremely erroneous and counterproductive (Iversen & Ghorpade, 2011).

Thus, the problem of child labour has to be solved by considering the multifarious aspects involved with it, including, but not limited to, familial structures, economic relations, social norms, marginalization, government policies, international discourses. Only by meaningfully engaging with these, child labour can be located in the intersectional marginalities. The structural inefficiencies and inequitable growth contribute considerably towards sustained burgeoning of the practices directly and indirectly linked to the prevalence of child labour.

**References**

Basu, K. (2003). The Economics of Child Labor. *Scientific American, 289*(4), 84-91.

Basu, K., & Tzannatos, Z. (2003). The Global Child Labor Problem: What Do We Know and What Can We Do? *The World Bank Economic Review, 17*(2), 147-173.

Basu, K., & Van, P. (1998). The Economics of Child Labor. *The American Economic Review, 88*(3), 412-427.

Bhukuth, A. (2008). Defining Child Labour: A Controversial Debate. *Development in Practice, 18*(3), 385-394.

Braun, S. (2006). Core Labour Standards and FDI: Friends or Foes? The Case of Child Labour. *Review of World Economics / Weltwirtschaftliches Archiv, 142*(4), 765-791.

Burra, N. (2001). Cultural Stereotypes and Household Behaviour: Girl Child Labour in India. *Economic and Political Weekly, 36*(5/6), 481-488.

Busse, M., & Braun, S. (2004). Export Structure, FDI and Child Labour. *Journal of Economic Integration, 19*(4), 804-829.

Chandrasekhar, C., & Ghosh, J. (2007). Recent Employment Trends in India and China: An Unfortunate Convergence? *Social Scientist, 35*(3/4), 19-46.

Chowdhury, S. (2011). Employment in India: What Does the Latest Data Show? *Economic and Political Weekly, 46*(32), 23-26.

Das, S., & Mukherjee, D. (2007). Role of women in schooling and child labour decision: the case of urban boys in india. *Social Indicators Research, 82*(3), 463-486.

DC, N., & Wind, S. (2009). Child labour in India: A Nexus among the State, Education and NGO? *The Indian Journal of Political Science, 70*(3), 825-838.

Doepke, M., & Zilibotti, F. (2009). International Labor Standards and the Political Economy of Child-Labor Regulation. *Journal of the European Economic Association, 7*(2/3), 508-518.

Emerson, P., & Knabb, S. (2013). Bounded rationality, expectations, and child labour. *The Canadian Journal of Economics / Revue Canadienne D'Economique, 46*(3), 900-927.

Iversen, V., & Ghorpade, Y. (2011). Misfortune, misfits and what the city gave and took: The stories of South-Indian child labour migrants 1935–2005. *Modern Asian Studies, 45*(5), 1177-1226.

Kovasevic, N. (2007). Child Slavery India's Self-Perpetuating Dilemma. *Harvard International Review, 29*(2), 36-39.

Lieten, G. (2002). Child Labour in India: Disentangling Essence and Solutions. *Economic and Political Weekly, 37*(52), 5190-5195.

Maurya, O. (2001). Child Labour in India. *Indian Journal of Industrial Relations, 36*(4), 492-498.

Mukherjee, D., & Das, S. (2008). Role of Parental Education in Schooling and Child Labour Decision: Urban India in the Last Decade. *Social Indicators Research, 89*(2), 305-322.

Ospina, E., & Roser, M. (2017). Child Labor. *OurWorldInData.org.*

Pande, R. (1996). Elimination of Child Labour: Use or Abuse? *Indian Journal of Industrial Relations, 32*(2), 216-222.

Rao, K., & Rao, M. (1998). Employers' View of Child Labour. *Indian Journal of Industrial Relations, 34*(1), 15-38.

Sumanta, L. (1980). Children without Childhood. *Economic and Political Weekly, 15*(23), 1007-1007.

Togunde, D., & Weber, E. (2007). Parents' views, children's voices: Intergenerational Analysis of Child Labor Persistence in Urban Nigeria. *International Journal of Sociology of the Family, 33*(2), 285-301.

Umapathy, G. (2017). Child Labour in Rural India . *IOSR Journal Of Humanities And Social Science , 22(7)*, 50-52.

Webbink, E., Smits, J., & De Jong, E. (2013). Household and Context Determinants of Child Labor in 221 Districts of 18 Developing Countries. *Social Indicators Research, 110*(2), 819-836.

Weiner, M. (1996). Child Labour in India: Putting Compulsory Primary Education on the Political Agenda. *Economic and Political Weekly, 31*(45/46), 3007-3014.

"Poverty is the worst form of violence" – Gandhi

"From each according to their ability, to each according to their need" – Marx

"Value of labour" is a problematic term. According to Marx (1844), this value is realized only when it is converted into a tangible product, because of the existence of capitalism as the dominant form of political economy. This has become the predicament of the labour. The labourer is no longer the determining agent of his own labour power but the capitalist and the products that is created by the labourer.

This is similar to the value of earth. There cannot be a defined value of earth. It depends on the location and also the resources that need to be exploited. For instance, land in Mumbai is far more expensive than in Jharkhand. But land in and around the gold mines of Jharkhand may be costlier than land in Mumbai. So, the subjectivity of "value" is extremely multidimensional.

Marx (1844) determined that in essence wages are determined through an antagonistic struggle between the capitalist and the worker. Almost always, the capitalist wins. The capitalist or the owner of the means of production can sustain for much longer without the workers, than the workers being able to sustain without them. This is because workers do not possess any of the surplus value that they produce. All of this surplus value is extracted and exploited by the capitalist, thus the worker has to depend on the owners of means of production for their daily sustenance through wages. Also, capitalists have been successful in forming cartels and being cooperative with one another, but this is not true for labour because the relationship between the labouring classes is always competitive. They want to get the work and wages even if it is at the cost of another labour. This is extremely problematic because these strategies have been successful in keeping the overall wages low for the labourers. This also provides the capitalists opportunity to earn even more profits by keeping the market wages low. This can be seen even in contemporaneous Indian milieu.

The capitalist and land owners have various other ways to have a monthly income other than the requisite wages, but the worker does not have any such cushion to fall back on.

The labouring class is dependent on its wages to run their homes and feed their families. Thus, they work for whatever wages is offered to them so that they do not die of starvation. This has both metaphorical and literal meaning. Workers at various hierarchies are paid below what their work deserves, at the lower levels the wages are actually starvation wages. But even if we see at the educated skilled levels, like the present case of Indian youth, even they are offered jobs by big corporations which are essentially hand to mouth existence. The capital owners and the land owners can earn interest and rents respectively, but the worker must necessarily toil to earn his wages. This is true even in the present day. This lack of resources amongst workers and the only way of sustenance through wages makes the competition among workers even fiercer.

Thus, the wages given to the working class is just for a "cattle-like existence". Smith (1776) calls this as the "ordinary wage"; this is compatible with the sustenance and reproduction of the labouring race. The demand and supply logic also holds true in case of labour, if the supply of workers far exceeds the demand for it, then a certain section of the labouring class will be condemned into "beggary and starvation". Thus, the worker is completely dependent on the capitalist for their mere survival. This, has changed slightly in the present context, because of the emergence of highly skilled jobs, like, say, computer coding or ethical hacking or neurosciences, the emergence of a highly skilled workforce can sometimes defy this supply demand logic. The demand can at times be more for certain highly skilled jobs. But in general, the capitalists have been successful in keeping the supply always greater than the demand, so that they can always hire at low wage rates and further their profits. This has been the case since the emergence of capitalism.

Also, to keep the prices of commodities close to its natural price it is important to manage the prices of land, labour, and capital, the factors of production. In order to achieve this, almost always the first factor of production which faces the axe is the labour head. This is also true in the present context, innovation, a buzzword of the present milieu has often been synonymous with cost cutting primarily owing to the decreased headcount. Although, it is claimed that innovation and technical advancement leads to the creation of jobs in many other new fields, it is important to examine how this is in accordance to the concept of division of labour. Nobody is against innovation and technological advancement, that is definitely important, but the problem is how do we make it inclusive and accessible to all. How to ensure that innovation is not necessarily synonymous to job loss but to new job creation. The most pertinent understanding which has to be developed is in a consumerist economy it is very important that people have the means to buy what is being produced. The economy does not function only on the thin aired speculations of the stock market, all the hot air results in crashes and economic downturns. This is of special importance in countries like India, with a huge population base of 1.3 billion, we have a ready market, and the only thing required is the purchasing power, which can be attained by giving the fair wages to the workers. Thus, logically putting things into perspective one can very well understand that when workers ask for better wages, it is not really a Marxist revolution, but instead it helps the consumerist capitalistic economy to further, but in a more inclusive and accessible fashion.

That has always been the objective; to provide a minimum decent standard of living for the whole populace. This can be achieved by giving the workers of the world their fair share of wages.

References

Smith, A. (1776). Wealth of Nations.

Marx, K. (1844). Economic and Philosophic Manuscripts of 1844.

<u>**9<sup>th</sup>. IndustriALL Global Union Action Plan 2016 – 2020**</u>

"A weak union is the biggest strength of any management"

- Sgt. S. K. Bhadra (Retd.)

The mission of this global action plan is to build a strong union power and defending the rights of the workers in all sectors. In any democratic country which espouses social equality, strong democratic unions are fundamental. IndustriALL is strengthened by its members. They organize, bargain, and campaign. The basic idea is that united workers are stronger, and IndustriALL serves as this voice of the workers. There is also a principled commitment towards transcending international borders and forming a workers' collective to confront global capital.

**Defending Workers' Rights**

IndustriALL has always been a fervent defender of workers' rights all over the world. It has employed all possible means to exert pressure on companies and governments which have violated workers' rights. Whenever, there has been any attack on workers and unions, IndustriALL has made use of its global alliances with various organizations to achieve its different goals.

The fight is against violations of inalienable rights of the workers, repression faced by unions, and extra-judicial killings.

The right to a living wage is also a fundamental action plan. The development and implementation of a national action plan and to build union capacity to fight for a living wage are going to be some mechanisms to achieve this objective. Promoting collective bargaining across industries as a means to introduce living wages to workers in MNC supply chains, building on the work done in global garment manufacturing chains. There are also on-going efforts to raise minimum wages to the level of living wages. The need for introduction of wage floors in countries without any is also of pertinent importance.

Women workers form a major part of this action plan, their rights will be protected and defended above all else. Since, they have been facing continual structural discrimination. There is also an increasing need to achieve safe and healthy working conditions for all workers and to pursue comprehensive health and safety provisions. Strong and enforceable regulatory frameworks are essential in this regard. Strict Occupational Health Safety measures and punitive penalties against any OHS violations are essential.

Governments are also being called upon to implement ILO conventions and for monitoring implementation by MNCs. The ratification of ILO Convention 76 on Safety and Health in Mines is also an important plank under this goal.

**Building Union Power**

The number one priority under this action plan is organizing and retaining members. The bargaining and legitimacy for any movement comes from industrial unions. To be the voice of workers, unions have to be a part of the process. Unions need to be developed as strong, democratic, independent, representative, and self-sustaining throughout the world. The divisions in the union movement must be meaningfully resolved and a unity has to be built. Union power at the national level enables the labour movement to defend and protect the political, social, and economic interests of the workers.

Small and divided unions weaken the whole labour movement. There are also plans to build unity amongst affiliates by various means like mergers, alliances, and creation of national councils. However, this unity must always be built on democratic principles and not on coercion, never on hegemony. IndustriALL does not provide affiliation to unions which work under the domination of employers or governments.

Policies and practices must always be transparent and democratic at all structural levels, like, global, regional, sectorial, and national levels. Cross border solidarity campaigns and recruitment have pertinent impacts on global supply chains. Unions from the global north and global south need to join forces in equal partnership to strengthen their organizations and increase capacity to represent workers. This includes, but is not limited to, industry unionism, viable systems of dues collection, union training, and changes in union structures and cultures to make sure that they function well. All workers especially women workers must find their rightful place in the union movement. Workers in precarious employments, informal workers, migrant workers, and unskilled workers must also be adequately represented because their contribution to the global economy is immense.

**Confronting Global Capital**

The voice of workers must be heard globally. Workers must have the power to influence the multinational corporations and institutions whose decisions and policies affect the lives of working people throughout the world, as workers and consumers. Workers must organize throughout the global operations and supply chains of MNCs. The deterioration of pay and working conditions in order to create exorbitant profits must be questioned. The UN Guiding Principles on Business and Human Rights are of considerable importance here.

There is also a need for constant and active dialogue with MNCs in order to build a strong industrial relations paradigm. This will enable the unions to raise their concerns at all levels of the company and across its supply chain. Various effective global agreements have been negotiated with MNCs with a focus on achieving secured work, organizing ability, job security, and ensuring collective bargaining rights are not coerced.

The Bangladesh Accord for Fire and Building Safety has opened up new possibilities for legally binding agreements with multiple MNCs to enforce compliance across an entire industry. The signatory MNCs then become legally obligated towards their commitments, this helps in addressing systemic rights violations at industry level.

IndustriALL also works with various other global unions to influence various global bodies like the International Monetary Fund, OECD, World Bank, G20, and other important international bodies. The advocacy is towards abandoning policies that perpetuate inequality and instead promote secure employment, labour rights, and living wages for all workers.

There is a sustained effort towards organizing and directing the power of trillions of dollars of workers capital away from speculative investments and towards investments that generate sustainable jobs. All investors must be held accountable for upholding workers' rights in MNCs and their supply chains. Developing proper strategies to mobilize workers' capital in order to influence corporate governance, investment, and enforcing international labour standards is also a major action plan. This will be done through alliances with socially responsible investors who would take punitive measures against companies that violate rights of the workers.

**Fighting Precarious Work**

Reaffirming the commitment to fight against precarious work in all its forms throughout the world and promoting direct contracts of unlimited duration is a major objective. There is a need to stop precarious work at all levels, globally, nationally, and regionally, in companies and in industries. There is also a plan to increase the awareness of the populace with regard to precarious work and how it undermines the rights of the workers. This has far reaching implications on the wellbeing of any society.

Precarious workers have to be organized into unions and their rights have to be secured by coordinated efforts at multi-level strategic actions. Governments must eliminate policies and legislations that encourage precarious work, and remove all legislative and other barriers that deny precarious workers their rights to join a union of their choice and bargain collectively. There has to be equal access to social protection for precarious workers. Political struggles against legislations which allow employers to employ and exploit precarious workers must also be supported.

Global unions must come together to pressurise the ILO to take action against precarious work. Particular importance must be given to ensure that precarious workers are able to exercise their rights of freedom of association and collective bargaining. Precarious work must be stopped at all levels of the supply chain. This also has to be advocated by institutions of global importance in policy and legal matters.

The world cannot accept a future where the youth are condemned to a lifetime of insecure jobs, without the protection of union membership. Employers must invest in young people through sustained long term training and education, employment contracts, and collectively bargained apprenticeship programs. The workers of the world cannot rest until all workers have access to a secure job with all their rights protected.

Promote Sustainable Industrial Policy

Industry is a fundamental prerequisite for jobs and development for national economies. It is also the foundation of good living standards. Therefore, strong industrial policies must be implemented which further social, economic, and environmental sustainability. However, any kind of economic progress and increase in productivity is beneficial if it is accompanied by social progress and environmental protection. Unions must work at the national level in engagement with the government and employers' associations to develop industrial policies that include such measures. The objectives for such policy decisions should be to safeguard and create well-paying jobs and secure employment opportunities which guarantees sustainable livelihood and employment.

Workers and unions working in the extractive, processing, and manufacturing industries have a critical role to play in this regard. The employees must have a say in the decisions that are taken by their industries. Unions especially in developing countries must endeavour towards industrial policies which enable workers and citizens to benefit from the exploitation of their own natural resources though value added processing and manufacturing. The promotion of skills transfer and technological advancement in line with the UN Sustainable Development Goals is an important action plan.

Working towards a fair, ambitious, and binding global treaty of climate change that takes into account social impacts and promotes the creation of green jobs is an important action plan for IndustriALL. Unions at the national level must work together with the government to take back power from the MNCs and their influencing abilities in determining the industrial development of a nation. Governments must ensure that profits are reinvested in research and development, training and skills enhancement. The emphasis should be on creating industrial policies which drive a more equitable distribution of the benefits of production towards the workers and society.

Tax loopholes must be plugged so that companies and corporations are compelled to support the development of local industries and infrastructure which they benefit from. Important decisions about the future of industries, jobs, and planet cannot be taken by multination companies and marketplaces; this power has to be taken back from them. A paradigm of sustainable industrial development which provides employment must be adopted and espoused for. The voices of the workers must be heard at all levels and for this to happen, workers of the world must unite.

<u>**10<sup>th</sup>. Land acquisition and involuntary resettlement – an ethical analysis**</u>

The objective of this paper is to analyse the phenomenon of "land acquisition and involuntary resettlement" from an ethical perspective. The particular theoretical and philosophical paradigms that would be used for this analysis are the consequentialist and deontological schools of thought.

A single line explanation for the consequentialist school of thought would be, "the end justifies the means". So the essence of the whole argument being made by the consequentialist school of thought has been encapsulated in that one line. Consequentialists like Demosthenes have elucidated that the morality of an act can only be judged in the event of a beneficial result.

But this is extremely problematic since the whole notion of "benefits" can itself be problematized, debated, and critiqued vigorously. This is because whose benefit are we talking about.

Let us now consider a case of a large Uranium mine near a community of villages. This Uranium site has been found only recently, but these communities have been living there for generations. The initiation of this Uranium mining site will destroy their natural habitats and occupations completely; leaving them completely livelihood-less. Moreover, most often than not they are forcefully evicted from their homes and lands, and forcibly resettled in tent houses, like how it has been done for thousands of victims of Narmada Dam Projects and many other dam projects around the country. Or you could also end up in sky-scraping slums, like how it is being done in Mahul, Mumbai. Both ways you are the one who is suffering. A common, innocent, vulnerable, honest Indian is the one who always suffers. Outside our academic papers and news articles lives and destinies of thousands are being altered, manipulated or destroyed. And here we are discussing about the ethical theories, the great ethical theories.

What are needed are structural changes. Whichever theory of ethics it is, a complete overhaul of the way we look at the issue of land acquisition is needed. I will soon try to shed some debunking light on the Deontological perspective as well. This perspective has often been claimed as the messiah for the Human Rights Approach, but sadly it is not. The problem with these theories is that they have been ideated and articulated in the swanky comforts of Oxford, Cambridge, JNU, TISS, etc. The actual world outside continues to suffer because we are no longer able to influence the policy making apparatus of this country. The nation is halfway gone to the dogs and halfway sold to the new age moneylenders (read WB, IMF, Defence Weapon Cartels, Private Lenders, etc.). The weapon supplying cartels (or corporations as they want to be referred as) are becoming ever powerful in this world where close to a billion people do not have food to eat and go hungry each day. So yes, the benefits and the concept of a "greater common good" has been a central argument given by consequentialists in support of such projects for land acquisition and voluntary resettlement. How many times does it happen that the people who are actually getting affected by the project, the people who are actually losing their lands, homes, generations of livelihood earning mechanism are consulted before taking actions and decisions for them?

When will we ever have a bottom-up approach rather than "pushing it down the throat" systemic structures of top-down approach? Hasn't the world yet understood that nothing, nothing that is ever forced on people actually survives for very long? People should be given their freedoms, also ensuring that their freedoms do not infringe upon others. This might sound very difficult theoretical, but doing this on the ground is actually very easy, if somebody has even the most basic sense of empathy, ethics, and competence they can achieve this easily.

So, a consequentialist would thus support the acquisition of land forcefully and resettling them involuntary. They would agree to this because the nuclear power produced by the extracted uranium will help provide electricity to a whole city. They would argue that the benefits to the environment and the continuous power supply to the city is reason enough to destroy these communities of villages. But for me doing this would be difficult. Since doing this would be giving the city population their rights by infringing or denying the rights of the village communities. If, hypothetically in this case by uprooting this village community of say 100 villages the government is able to provide clean nuclear fuel to all the cities and villages in India then it is fine to acquire the land and proceed with the project, because in this case the benefits far outweigh the costs. But, suppose for providing power to each city in India, a community of 100 villages have to be uprooted then that cannot and ought not to happen in this nation. So, this would be my approach to dealing with this problem. A contextualized, community decided, subjective and qualitatively varied solution. This is what I would like to call a "pragmatic-idealist" framework for ethics.

Now examining the deontological perspective, this school of thought generally propounds that if a certain action is undertaken after properly following the rules and regulations, they are moral and ethical. This sounds like a theory propounded by the Indian bureaucrats; because their obsession with rules and regulations ultimately culminating in a huge conundrum of bureaucratic red tapism sounds like the foundation of this theory, epitomized by the ultimate License Raj, which once terrified all commerce in the country. So, just having rules and regulations need not always translate into moral and ethical actions. Considering the above example itself, suppose all rules and regulations are followed for their forceful land acquisition and involuntary resettlement, will that make the project ethical and moral? I definitely believe in the nugatory. Instead it might end up providing a blue print for all such future projects.

Another important issue which merits our thought and introspective contemplation is the idea of justified and unjustified demand. This is another area where many theorists and policy luminaires have failed to provide any meaningful solution. For example, a tribal farmer is going to lose 1 acre of his personal land which is on his name, and access to a common property resource of 1000 acres. The livelihood of his/her family is equally dependent on both of these claims. Now is he/she unjustified in asking for a 5 acre plot for agriculture where she is being resettled? Have we become so blind that we cannot see the logic behind that claim?

Now, suppose an illegal slum dweller living over a floodwater drain is involuntarily relocated to a high-rise slum (the likes you will find in Mumbai), is s/he justified if s/he claims that s/he wants a 4 BHK flat in Colaba? Obviously not, but what merits our pertinent attention is the fact that marginalized or underserved people never ask for such flamboyance and pompous needs, they just ask for a minimum basic standard of living, which is otherwise known as "a dignified living", a popular concept in most of the Nordic nations and western developed nations with high HDI rankings. Also, resettlement in cities or otherwise too must implement the concept of housing based on family needs and size. For example, this has been ideated at the Azim Premji University that all staff both academic and non-academic would be given housing on campus. The most striking feature of this housing plan was that the staff would be given housing based on the number of members in their family not based on the designation that they are working as. So, if an office attendant has an 8 member family, then s/he would be given a 4BHK house; and if the Vice Chancellor is a bachelor/spinster and lives alone then s/he/they would be given a 1BHK flat. This is something which is an interesting concept and has to be articulated in policy making.

Thus, I hope that serious changes are brought into the land acquisition project implementation frameworks in our country. I hope the people who have been wronged in the past by their country (or more aptly the government, an expression of the country) get their rightful dues and timely justice.

# 11<sup>th</sup>. Marketing Strategy for Organic Farm Products

This paper endeavours to develop a marketing strategy for organic farm products, "Farmer's Fresh" These will be produced by farmers' collectives and they will own the company. All the profits would be shared amongst them. The marketing division of the company will be a wholly owned subsidiary of the company.

The first step in the marketing strategy will begin by problematizing the existing farm products being consumed by Indians. The second step would be aggressive branding and online campaigning to build a nationwide visibility and initiating a movement to eat pure and affordable organics, providing the solution to the existing problem. The third step would be to directly engage with business to business channels for sales through retailers. The fourth step is engaging with large scale customers like universities, colleges, and corporate offices where we can get large scale orders. The fifth step would be to build visibility by direct marketing strategies. The fifth step would be to start the discourse on how the company is completely different and new, how it is completely owned by farmers eliminating the need for middlemen, this would start a nationwide discourse on prior unknown or unutilized models of business, government figures or other stakeholders can be involved in this step. The sixth step and the unique selling proposition for our company would be the absolute transparency and accountability that we will offer by providing the QR codes on packet to enable the customers to see and feel the process of growing what is there on their plates (has been explained in the later paragraphs). This is absolutely unique and this might start a policy trend to make supply chains more sustainable specially in the developing worlds.

The pilot project will be started in Mumbai and then will be extended all over the country. Specific focus will also be given towards targeting the universities, colleges, and their dining hall committees. Apart from this all large consumers would also be targeted. This will be done so that large customers can be attained with relative pace enabling the business to reach break-even points quickly or even to see and realize profits, further enabling the business to expand aggressively in other locations. So, larger customers if attained in the beginning can help in providing the base further expansions something similar to economies of scale and increasing returns to scale. The large demand orders can provide the required numbers for the company to survive and expand.

So "we" (the marketing team supported by all the other teams of the company) will start by aggressively problematizing the existing food products being consumed by students, office goers, and all people in general. We will focus on students and office-goers in particular because they consume a large amount of internet based digital content, and our marketing strategies will be able to easily permeate to them. They would be the first wave of customers whom we will target since they can be easily reached. We will bring forth various research studies which will show the amount of pesticides and fertilizers coming on to our plates and its ill effects. We will also show how a lot of vegetables are grown on the Mumbai railway tracks and end up on the plates of unquestioning individuals who might have bought those items from big malls.

We will brand the product as "Farmer's Fresh". This will be accompanied by aggressive branding. We will have QR codes on the packets of the farm products wherein they can go on a webpage which will show the farmer and farming procedures that have been used to grow that particular vegetable, grain, or fruit. A direct link will be established between the farmer and the consumer. We will not have single video for each product but for thousands or lakhs of kilograms of products there will be a single video, if the products are same. For different products there will be different videos. Proper and detailed nuances will be decided after extensive brainstorming on making this unique selling proposition as truly path breaking.

What is surprising is that, there is not a single initiative that has been taken like this. Although, there are certain organic brands existing in the market they are mostly too expensive, marketed very less, or have zero branding efforts. Also, the customers can never really be sure whether the organic products are really organic or not. Not a single product in the market whether in farming or in any FMCG product category has thought of providing a QR code to show their manufacturing processes. The true connect with the consumers is somewhere missing. With the whole discourse on sustainability and consuming organic catching up steam, this field will surely shape up a lot of future market activities. We will be the pioneers in this marketing strategy. We will bring complete transparency and accountability, connecting the consumers with the producers.

The connection between the farmer and the customer will be completely real. Since there will be no middle men the cost of the products will also be less, perhaps even lesser than regular items. Initially we will have certain overhead costs to setup the digital initiatives and to get the basic supply chain management mechanisms in place, like cold storage facilities, etc. We will get these facilities or the harvesting season inaugurated by a Union or State Minister of Agriculture so that it will give added limelight to the company. They would also be willing to come to such events since this is a farmers' collective and not a conventional profit making company. The journey will not be easy because organizing the farmers into collectives and making them grow products without fertilizers or pesticides can be difficult. But when they understand the potential of this initiative I am sure they would be happy to come on-board. The profits from this would be something that farmers would have never seen in their lives because they would be the real owners of the company and all the profits would be shared by them after taking care of the future business needs. The various teams including the marketing teams, branding teams, supply management, sales teams, etc. would be employees who would be paid salaries. They would bring in their intellectual capital into the company to help it prosper.

Such an initiative is non-existent in the country. We will take our organic products which will have no pesticides or fertilizers to each and every kitchen in the country. We will have aggressive online campaigning, direct campaigning by getting on roads, doing road-shows, going to malls and putting up marketing stalls, going to retail outlets and building visibility, directly indulging in business to business sales to retailers, etc. These would be some of the conventional marketing strategies that we will implement along with our revolutionary new methods.

But more than this we will try to completely change the existing paradigm in the agricultural product arena. Our direct connection between the consumers and the farmers on the field by leveraging the potential of technology and the digital India initiatives will be some of the reasons for the success of our marketing strategy.

Brief description about the geographical locations that we will be targeting for the product:

First we will begin in Mumbai. It is the financial capital of India. We will begin here because of the existence of large scale customers whom we can target initially. Next we can focus on Pune (because of proximity and a large target population), Bangalore, Delhi, and once we have enough market base and a sound balance sheet we can aggressively get into smaller Indian geographies, providing organic food to as many Indians as possible. By large scale customers in these cities I mean colleges, universities, corporate offices, etc. where the food for hundreds or thousands is cooked. In these places we can involve twin marketing strategies. One is directly impacting the end users, that is, students or office goers. We can directly and aggressively target them through online or direct channels and completely make them believe that whatever they are eating is dangerous for them and for their health so they must switch to organic products from "Farmer's Fresh". This would lead to the pressures on the management to turn towards procurement of organic products. We will provide them with branding and merchandising in the dining spaces to show that they are using our organic products. I do realize that this might be negatively detrimental to the existing farmers in the short run, which is a major concern for the company as well, but there will be a quick on-boarding process for interested farmers. Wherein, they can get on-board with our company in a matter of few hours after some basic paper works. They would do away with their use of pesticides and fertilizers (which is beneficial for them as well) and start using organic techniques and our farming team of the company will help them in the complete procedure. For the period between sowing and the first harvest they would also be provided with monetary assistance from the company.

Basically, all the multifarious problems that might arise will be dealt with keeping in mind the principles of equity, justice, sustainability, inclusiveness, and dignity, certain principles which seem to be missing from the dictionaries of present business strategy leaders and marketing experts.

Mumbai has a population of around 2 crore. It has a megacity area of 603 square kilometres. This translates to a population density of 21000 per square kilometre, highest in the country. The total GDP of Mumbai is around $400 billion, and that of India is $2 trillion dollars. That means around $1/5^{th}$ of the total Indian GDP emanates from Mumbai. Now, considering the whole of India, the total population is 130 crore, making it the second most populous country in the world. Thus, the market potential in this country is extraordinarily colossal. India is also a largely consumption driven economy so finding customers for something as basic as food will not be that difficult either. Organic food consumption will be revolutionary with the correct marketing tools and focus on scalability and affordability.

We have to focus on matching the 4 C's with the 4 P's of marketing. In this model we match the consumer needs and wants with the product being offered, costs to price, convenience to the place or ease of buying (in this we can leverage the online home delivery model, making it even more lucrative), communication and promotion.

If properly implemented this product and marketing strategy could be truly revolutionary.

**List of abbreviations**

| | |
|---|---|
| BIMARU | Bihar, Madhya Pradesh, Rajasthan, Uttar Pradesh |
| GDP | Gross Domestic Product |
| HDI | Human Development Index |
| ILO | International Labour Organization |
| IMF | International Monetary Fund |
| MGNREGA | Mahatma Gandhi National Rural Employment Guarantee Act |
| MP | Madhya Pradesh |
| UN | United Nations |
| UNO | United Nations Organization |
| UP | Uttar Pradesh |
| WB | World Bank |
| WTO | World Trade Organization |

**Introduction**

The objective of this paper is to elucidate that the neoliberal state is not willingly interested to offer "social protection" (Standing, 2007) to its citizens on a universal basis. Whatever forms of social protection does exist in the contemporaneous milieu is inadequate and also at threat of diminishing further (Bernhard, 2010), due to the interests of the neoliberal stakeholders who maliciously form the state and control its polity (Tambunan, 2003). Thus, the interests of a neoliberal state are fundamentally antagonistic to the welfare of its citizens. This however is carefully concealed from the general discourse whilst manipulating the global political economy to benefit a few developed countries (which themselves have high inequality) (Gwynne & Kay, 2000), zillionaires (and their corporations, which are now "humans" in their own standing) (Ahmed, 2010), and financial institutions at the cost of billions of hapless individuals (Rodgers, 2011; Haque, 2008).

Social protection is understood as a policy instrument which was traditionally utilized to protect the citizens and households from contingencies like illness (Elias, 2007), job loss or unemployment (Guha, 2009), economic crises (Hirway & Shah, 2011; Freeland, 2013). It can also be used to enable people to cope with certain other conditions like loss of livelihoods (Sundar, 2005), absence of low levels of income (Murayama & Yokota, 2009), resource poverty (Oommen, 2009), absence of decent work (Palo et al., 2000), etc. The term social protection is all encompassing and therefore has been interpreted differently in different contexts (Panic, 2007). But what remains a difficult proposition to be decided is whether they have been correctly contextualized or not. Many European countries are facing austerity drives on social protection mechanisms. These were considered as the mecca for welfare states and social protection policies but with the increasing demonization of social protection in countries like the United States of America (USA), where the social protection recipients are looked down upon, the discourse is soon changing (Jinkings & Guimaraes, 2011; Robinson, 1994). Indian policymakers have to understand that no amount of economic growth will be able to truly develop India if that growth is non-inclusive and iniquitous (Ratnam, 2000; Sehgal, 2005).

**Defining the concept**

"Social Protection" is often seen as an umbrella term used for a variety of policies and programmes. It is often interchangeably used with another term "social security"; although, the two are different concepts (Standing, 2007). ILO also differentiates between the two, social protection being much broader of the two. In most of the developed countries social protection generally comprises of social insurance (contributory programmes covering various contingencies) (Hirway & Shah, 2011), social assistance (tax-financed initiatives and programmes for poverty and vulnerability alleviation) (Gooptu, 2009), and employment programmes (active or passive) (Garg, 2005). Social safety nets are another set of ideas which come under the domain of social protection. However the nets are only short term buffers to mitigate the immediate vulnerabilities (Devereux & Sabates, 2007; Day, 2009).

Social protection is a combination of formal and informal initiatives which provide income or in-kind transfers or combinations of both along with other measures to poor and vulnerable households (Freeland, 2013; Sen et al., 1991). This is primarily done to: act as a safety net for the extremely poor, protecting people against risks and livelihood shocks, enabling people out of poverty, supporting social justice and greater equitability in society (Chakrabarti & Dasgupta, 2007). Social protection thus combines the various public actions taken to respond effectively against different levels of vulnerability, risk, and deprivations that are considered as socially unacceptable in the given contexts (Bullock, 2009; Andersen, 1990).


**Social protection and underlying motivations**

The reasons for endorsing or promoting social protection in developing countries can have various underlying motivations. Some have classified this into two groups: instrumentalists and activists (Devereux & Sabates, 2007). The instrumentalists opine that extreme vulnerability and poverty undermines the achievement of the developmental goals (Boss, 1988). They propose for mechanisms to bring in private insurance players and the ability of the market. The activists on the other hand consider extreme inequality and abject poverty as symptoms of structurally iniquitous conditions and social injustice (Papola, 2011; Sinha, 2004). They believe that welfare programmes are the necessary steps that need to be taken for achieving the ideals of a universal social minimum. Here, the entitlements extend beyond cash and food transfers, they lead to a system based on citizenship and not philanthropy. This is similar to a rights based approach, where no individual is excluded from access to social security because of their sex, age, marital status, ethnicity, etcetera (Freeland, 2013).

Decent work and social protection are fundamental elements which ensure a basic standard of living and drive inclusive and sustainable growth. Articles 22 and 25 of the Universal Declaration of Human Rights have recognized the right to social protection for all members of society (Routh, 2011; John, 2003). Although, in principle nobody disagrees with this provision, the means of reaching the end is different for different individuals and organizations. Thus, their advocacy also differs. The most principal of all disagreements is whether social protection should be universal or targeted?

There is a fundamental difference between a "universalist" approach and a "neo-liberal, small state" approach. The ILO is a strong proponent of the Universalist approach to social protection. It aims not only for removal of abject poverty and vulnerabilities but also eradicating inequality. Accordingly, the concepts of "minimum global social protection floor" and a minimum universal basic income have been introduced (Standing, 2008; Freeland, 2013). This model proposes for giving money and cash transfers instead of providing services. The probability of implementing these concepts in Toto is actually very less.

Counter-intuitively, the World Bank vociferously vouches for the neoliberal small-state approach. It believes that resources are scant and therefore social protection must be focussed on the poorest of the poor. Often targeting to the poor is ineffective because of the existence of "clogged pipes" (Jhabvala & Standing, 2010). Clogged pipes are metaphorically denoting the structural inefficiencies and pervasive corruption along with a general apathy for the poor. It also argues that the "beneficiaries" must do something in exchange for the benefits that they receive. Some of the popular examples for such schemes are Latin American programmes, Ethiopia's Productive Safety Net Programme, Indonesia's Program "Keluarga Harapan", and Pakistan's Benazir Income Support Programme (Jonakin, 2006). The famous MGNREGA Act of India can also be considered as one of such programmes (Gupta, 2011).

**Shifting patterns**

There has been a trend of shifting social policies from being universal to being targeted since the 1980s (Jinkings & Guimaraes, 2011; Robinson, 1994). This can be seen in both developed and developing countries (John, 2003). This shift was observed with an overall change in the ideation of a welfare state (Day, 2009). Over time the debate between universalist and targeted social protection has become theoretical. Since, both of these cannot operate in silos while completely ignoring the other. Certain elements of each are combined to make effective working programmes (Devereux & Sabates, 2007). Also, political gains can largely influence many social protection policies as can be popularly seen in Indian contexts (Bardhan, 1977). Proponents of targeting have argued that if social protection is to work and ultimately reduce poverty then one has to know who is poor and why (Ahmed, 2010).

Privatization of health care and pensions has contributed towards further accentuation of social inequalities. Markets have not been the best equalizers when it comes to the question of social protection. Since majority of these plans are employment linked, they tend to be highly individualized and heftily priced. It also does not do justice to labour market inequalities like wage differentials between genders (Vijayabaskar, 2011; Sangari, 2015).

Another major problem is that social protection is often linked to formal employment. This is extremely problematic for developing countries which have a large share of its population working in the informal sector. Thus, by definition it becomes exclusionary for the overwhelming majority of the population (Jonakin, 2006; Papola, 1994; Erumban, 2009).

Paying for the social protection bills is an arena of long ensuing tussles. The dominant international hegemons have decreed states to lower their deficits; this has resulted in poorer states completely doing away with social protection policies since they cost huge bills (Haque, 2008). Also, the percentage of population reeling under poverty in poorer nations is so large that it becomes financially impossible for them to implement meaningful social protection policies (Elias, 2007; Phukon, 2008).

One fact which cannot be refuted by anyone is the pivotal role of the state in implementation of social protection policies. The state is the primary guarantor of a decent and dignified life which can be attained through social protection of the citizenry.

The state must also endeavour to provide a minimum basic standard of living. To have effective and efficient social protection regimes the state must be responsible in providing finance, regulations, administration, and institutional rigour for the programmes. However, the reality remains that the poorest of individuals in the developing countries seek support from non-state actors the majority of times. This includes, but is not limited to, kin, community, and religious institutions.

**Challenges to social protection**

Three major challenges in implementing social protection policies at the country level have been identified by various international bodies. First, the domestic expenses for introducing social protection can be simply beyond the financial capacity of countries having large populations living below poverty (Bardhan, 1989). Second, the risk of future rise in the cost of social protection provisions due to unforeseen exigencies like natural disasters, epidemics, loss of export markets could lead to great national crises (Yuan et al., 2009; Dutta, 2007). Third, with the rights based approach the state could face legal claims for non-provision of certain social protections (Sharma, 2006; Bhattacharya, 2002).

However, strongly rebuking such arguments, the ILO has claimed that the cost for providing social protection to all of the world's poor would be actually less than 2% of the world GDP. But this does not discount the fact that poorer countries actually face severe financial constraints in implementing meaningful social protection regimes. To mitigate this problem there were UN efforts to create a worldwide fund for social protection which could be used by countries in need but because of political and strategic economic differences amongst countries this could not be implemented (Chandrasekhar, 2011).

From the coding structure of NSSO (National Sample Survey Organisation), there are five instruments of social security: Provident Fund (PF), Pension, Gratuity, Health Care and Maternity Benefit. While percentage of employed persons in rural areas without any social security entitlement is 97%, this proportion is 79% in urban area (Oommen, 2009; Papola, 2011).

**The case for a global social protection floor**

ILO (2011) propounded the idea of a "social protection floor" – this meant that no individual should "live below a certain income level", and everyone must have "access to essential public services", like sanitation, water, health, and education (Cichon & Hagemejer, 2007). ILO has been developing this idea of a social protection floor from a long time. It envisages basic social security provisions for all humans and thus lays the groundwork for a universal social protection regime. It involves income security like pensions and unemployment benefits along with universal access to social services like health care provisions, educational infrastructure, nutrition, and affordable housing (Rodgers, 2011).

ILO has developed a twin-pronged strategy to achieve this. First, is the guaranteed universal access to essential services like health and income security (Standing, 1997), also known as the horizontal dimension. The second is the progressive achievement of higher levels of protection; this is known as the vertical dimension. Thus, the contextual settings will change with each country even within the global social protection floor framework. There also might be new socio-economic classes which might be formed (Standing, 2014).

There is a growing consensus that social protection floor is required for investment in human capital. Many with vested interests have tried to oppose it claiming a variety of reasons. The Western powers are significantly uninterested in providing social protection floors to the poorest of countries fearing that it might have financial repercussions for them (Scheuerman, 2001). Severe austerity measures have negatively impacted the social protection schemes even within Europe.

**Conclusion and analysis**

Neoliberal states adopt strategies which try to maintain social order and safeguard public property by systemic economic deregulation and increasing social precariousness (Standing, 2014). They have been one of the principal forces behind the destruction of the welfare state (Chakrabarti & Dasgupta, 2007; Andersen, 1990), aggravating poverty (Bullock, 2009; Sen et al., 1991), despotic structural inefficiencies (Ahmed, 2010), and intolerant hierarchical governance frameworks which deprive the common masses from meaningful forms of social protections while being subject to widespread repression (Chandrasekhar, 2011). Lack of social protection causes social insecurity which makes repression easier (Garg, 2005).

In recent international discourses "social protection" has become one of the catch phrases for anchoring discussions and debates (Standing, 2007). However, different organizations use it differently, often burdened by their ideological leanings.

Social protection in today's neoliberal world is a "global challenger" (Bernhard, 2010). The classic questions that still debilitate the central debate are – who are the "true" beneficiaries that must be benefitted from such policies, and who should pay for the funding of these policies? However, it is pertinent to mention that only about 1/4th of the total world population actually avails of any kind of social protection benefits. Of those availing some form of social protection, a large proportion of them are in the developed nations, fewer in the developing nations, and the condition of the less developed nations are appalling. Thus, there is a need to increase access to the social protection mechanisms. The problems that social protection policies face largely revolve around the issues of whether they should be universal or targeted, who is to finance them, how are they to be implemented, what are the pre-requisites to be eligible for certain policies.

Neoliberalism has become the dominant and hegemonic archetype for all policy instrumentation paradigms at the global level (Tambunan, 2003). This policy paradigm has been able to transverse economic, social, and cultural policy in all parts of the world, including the first and third world nations. The chief proponents of this neoliberal structural hegemony have been the International Monetary Fund (IMF), the World Bank (WB), and the World Trade Organization (WTO) among others. These have successfully permeated into the economic, monetary, and fiscal policies of almost all countries without taking into consideration the root cause of poverty and resource deprivation. The social protection measures taken by such governance mechanisms have been inadequate in dealing with the inherent deficiencies. People have not been able to utilize such social protection policies to make their lives better. The idea of a "welfare state" in most of these countries has been a sham (Rodgers, 2011). But what merits attention here is that the traditional western capitalist societies have performed way better at providing its citizens a decent life and minimum basic standard of living, when compared to the developing and less developed world, whose performance in this regard has been abysmal. Although, civil society organizations, NGOs, academics, think tanks have often tried to bring out this dichotomy between the envisaged social protections and the actual needs of the people, they have not been able to accomplish any substantial objectives. Their actions have been able to only elicit lackadaisical responses from the state and its functionaries (Sangari, 2015).

Thus, there exists a certain dissonance between the social protection policies of the state and the real poverty alleviation requirements of the people (Sinha, 2004). This is considering the countries where social protection is actually provided by the state. In many other countries the provisions for social protection are not even formulated or implemented. If we consider the case of India, we can see that some states have been able to perform well to provide various social protections to its citizens and this has also improved their Human Development Index (HDI) rankings, like Tamil Nadu, Kerala. But the performance by some other states is appalling, like Bihar, Odisha. The popular acronym given by Ashish Bose (1985), BIMARU, for the states of Bihar, Madhya Pradesh (MP), Rajasthan, and Uttar Pradesh (UP), still holds true to a certain extent. Even within these states there are widespread inequalities. No society in India is homogeneous. All demographics are extremely heterogeneous and these are not generalizations for the whole states. But the presence of abject poverty in these states is a concern which social protection policies must address (Papola, 2011).

Furthermore, the neoliberal policy analysts are astute in changing the definition of poverty as per their convenience. The use of parlance like poverty, resource poor, vulnerable, at risk, has become increasingly popular to keep the general populace in a sense of constant bemusement. The terms have been manipulated to an extent that the real meaning often gets smeared. Standing (2007) has critiqued this politics and manipulation of language. These changes in definitions and eligibility criteria for being declared as eligible for social protection or not is extremely problematic for the people who are actually in need for such policies.

Significant intellectual backing for such changes in definitions and eligibility criterions are provided by the international bodies which are then emulated by the respective governments. In the Indian case this can be seen by another level of fragmentation, one where the central planning bodies make policies which are then implemented by the state level bodies. This is problematic since it is the conventional top-down approach without considering the actual needs of the bottom and most importantly the voices from the margins. The prevalence of an unholy nexus between the state, capitalists, and certain civil society agents to systematically impoverish the already marginalized citizenry cannot be denied.

**References**

Ahmad, E., Drèze, J., Hills, J. & Sen, A. (Eds.) (1991). *Social Security in Developing Countries*. Oxford: Clarendon Press.

Ahmed, W. (2010). Neoliberalism, Corporations, and Power: Enron in India. *Annals of the Association of American Geographers, 100*(3), 621-639.

Alakh N. Sharma. (2006). Flexibility, Employment and Labour Market Reforms in India. *Economic and Political Weekly, 41*(21), 2078-2085.

Andersen, G. E. (1990). The Three Worlds of Welfare Capitalism. USA: Blackwell.

Anjan Chakrabarti, & Byasdeb Dasgupta. (2007). Disinterring the Report of National Commission on Labour: A Marxist Perspective.*Economic and Political Weekly, 42*(21), 1958-1965.

Athukorala, P., Fukao, K., & Yuan, T. (2009). Economic transition and labour market integration in China. In Garnaut R., Song L., & Woo W. (Eds.), *China's New Place in a World in Crisis: Economic, Geopolitical and Environmental Dimensions* (pp. 179-208). ANU Press.

Bardhan, K. (1977). Rural Employment, Wages and Labour Markets in India: A Survey of Research: III. *Economic and Political Weekly, 12*(28), 1101-1118.

Bardhan, K. (1989). Poverty, Growth and Rural Labour Markets in India. *Economic and Political Weekly, 24*(12), A21-A38.

Bhattacharyya, D. (2002). WTO and Indian Labour. *Indian Journal of Industrial Relations, 37*(4), 579-592.

Boss, H. (1988). Division of Labour and Unproductive Labour In a System of Natural Liberty: Adam Smith's Dilemma. *Historical Reflections / Réflexions Historiques, 15*(2), 417-442.

Bullock, I. (2009). The Rise and Fall of New Labour? A Social Democracy for 21st Century Britain? *Labour / Le Travail, 64*, 173-191.

Chandrasekhar, C. (2011). Notes on Neoliberalism and the Future of the Left. *Social Scientist, 39*(1/2), 20-34.

Cichon, M. & Hagemejer, K. (2007). Investing in a social security floor for all. *International Social Security Review*, 60, 169-196.

Day, P. (2009). A new history of social welfare. USA, Boston, Pearson.

Devereux, S. & Sabates, R. (2007). Editorial Introduction: Debating Social Protection. *IDS Bulletin*, 38(3): p. 1-7.

Dutta, P. (2007). Trade Protection and Industry Wages in India.*Industrial and Labor

*Relations Review, 60*(2), 268-286.

Elias, J. (2007). Women Workers and Labour Standards: The Problem of 'Human Rights'. *Review of International Studies, 33*(1), 45-57.

Erumban, A. (2009). Productivity and Unit Labour Cost in Indian Manufacturing: A Comparative Perspective. *Economic and Political Weekly, 44*(15), 39-48.

Freeland, N. (2013). The Seven Deadly Myths of Social Protection. *Pathways' Perspectives on social policy in international development*, 10:1

Garg, P. (2005). Globalization : Its Impact On Labour. *The Indian Journal of Political Science, 66*(4), 813-830.

Gooptu, N. (2009). Neoliberal Subjectivity, Enterprise Culture and New Workplaces: Organised Retail and Shopping Malls in India. *Economic and Political Weekly, 44*(22), 45-54.

Guha, A. (2009). Labour Market Flexibility: An Empirical Inquiry into Neoliberal Propositions. *Economic and Political Weekly,44*(19), 45-52.

Gupta, B. (2011). Wages, unions, and labour productivity: Evidence from Indian cotton mills. *The Economic History Review,64*(S1), 76-98.

Standing, G. (1980). Basic Needs and the Division of Labour. *The Pakistan Development Review, 19*(3), 211-235.

Gwynne, R., & Kay, C. (2000). Views from the Periphery: Futures of Neoliberalism in Latin America. *Third World Quarterly, 21*(1), 141-156.

Haque, M. (2008). Global Rise Of Neoliberal State And Its Impact On Citizenship: Experiences In Developing Nations. *Asian Journal of Social Science, 36*(1), 11-34.

Hirway, I., & Shah, N. (2011). Labour and Employment in Gujarat. *Economic and Political Weekly, 46*(44/45), 62-64.

Hirway, I., & Shah, N. (2011). Labour and Employment under Globalisation: The Case of Gujarat. *Economic and Political Weekly, 46*(22), 57-65.

Jhabvala, R., & Standing, G. (2010). Targeting to the 'Poor': Clogged Pipes and Bureaucratic Blinkers. *Economic and Political Weekly, 45*(26/27), 239-246.

Jinkings, I., & Guimarães, V. (2011). The Neoliberal State and the Penalization of Misery. *Latin American Perspectives, 38*(5), 9-18. Retrieved from http://www.jstor.org/stable/23060117

John, J. (2003). Labour scene in India. *International Union Rights, 10*(4), 9-11.

Jonakin, J. (2006). Cycling between Vice and Virtue: Assessing the Informal Sector's Awkward Role under Neoliberal Reform.*Review of International Political*

*Economy, 13*(2), 290-312.

Sundar, K. R. S. (2005). Labour Flexibility Debate in India: A Comprehensive Review and Some Suggestions. *Economic and Political Weekly, 40*(22/23), 2274-2285.

Murayama, M., & Yokota, N. (2009). Revisiting Labour and Gender Issues in Export Processing Zones: Cases of South Korea, Bangladesh and India. *Economic and Political Weekly,44*(22), 73-83.

Oommen, T. (2009). Indian Labour Movement: Colonial Era to the Global Age. *Economic and Political Weekly, 44*(52), 81-89.

Palo, S., Padhi, N., & Panigrahi, S. (2000). Labour Standards in the Aftermath of Structural Adjustment Programme: The Case of India. *Indian Journal of Industrial Relations, 35*(3), 381-398.

Panić, M. (2007). Does Europe need neoliberal reforms?*Cambridge Journal of Economics, 31*(1), 145-169.

Papola, T. (1994). Employment Growth and Social Protection of Labour in India. *Indian Journal of Industrial Relations, 30*(2), 117-143.

Papola, T. (2011). Employment in Development: Connection between Indian Strategy and ILO Policy Agenda. *Economic and Political Weekly, 46*(10), 62-67.

Phukon, D. (2008). Gender development approach and social protection : Understanding the Case of Assam. *The Indian Journal of Political Science, 69*(4), 771-785.

Pravin Sinha. (2004). Representing Labour in India. *Development in Practice, 14*(1/2), 127-135.

Rakhi Sehgal. (2005). Social Reproduction of Third World Labour in the Era of Globalisation: State, Market and the Household. *Economic and Political Weekly, 40*(22/23), 2286-2294.

Ratnam, C. (2000). India and International Labour Standards. *Indian Journal of Industrial Relations, 35*(4), 461-485.

Robinson, I. (1994). NAFTA, Social Unionism, and Labour Movement Power in Canada and the United States. *Relations Industrielles / Industrial Relations, 49*(4), 657-695.

Rodgers, G. (2011). India, the ILO and the Quest for Social Justice since 1919. *Economic and Political Weekly, 46*(10), 45-52.

Routh, S. (2011). The Judiciary and (Labour) Law in the Development Discourse in India. *Verfassung Und Recht in Übersee / Law and Politics in Africa, Asia and Latin America,44*(2), 237-257.

Sangari, K. (2015). To Market, To Market: Gendered Contradictions. *Social*

*Scientist, 43*(9/10), 29-40.

Scheuerman, W. (2001). False Humanitarianism?: US Advocacy of Transnational Labour Protections. *Review of International Political Economy, 8*(3), 359-388.

Standing, G. (1997). The Folly of Social Safety Nets: Why Basic Income Is Needed in Eastern Europe. *Social Research, 64*(4), 1339-1379.

Standing, G. (2007). Social Protection. *Development in Practice,17*(4/5), 511-522.

Standing, G. (2008). Economic Insecurity and Global Casualisation: Threat or Promise? *Social Indicators Research,88*(1), 15-30.

Standing, G. (2014). The precariat. *Contexts, 13*(4), 10-12.

Stefan Bernhard. (2010). From conflict to consensus: European neoliberalism and the debate on the future of EU social policy. *Work Organisation, Labour & Globalisation, 4*(1), 175-192.

Tambunan, R. (2003). A neoliberal threat. *International Union Rights, 10*(3), 27-27.

Vijayabaskar, M. (2011). Global Crises, Welfare Provision and Coping Strategies of Labour in Tiruppur. *Economic and Political Weekly, 46*(22), 38-45.

Index

List of abbreviations



References

List of abbreviations

| ABRR | Annual Business Responsive Reports |
|------|------------------------------------|
| BSE  | Bombay Stock Exchange |
| CSR  | Corporate Social Responsibility |
| GDP  | Gross Domestic Product |
| MCA  | Ministry of Corporate Affairs |
| NGO  | Non-Governmental Organizations |
| NSE  | National Stock Exchange |
| NVG  | National Voluntary Guidelines |
| PPP  | Purchasing Power Parity |
| US   | United States |

*This paper will define and explain the various concepts involved in the topic. It will elucidate the multiple nuances inherently involved in them. It will also look at the various technicalities. The interlinkages between them have also been examined. Along with the implications for labour, a "labourist" perspective is utilized for the critical analysis. NVGs, ABRR, CSR, and Trade Union Strategies in dealing with these are the prominent topics that will be dealt with.*

## Introduction

Business is about people, making their lives better; this is one of the principal objectives of any business (Epstein, 1989). The need for sustainability in the contemporaneous milieu is pertinent (Braithwaite, 2017; Baines, 2009). This sustainability is multifarious in nature – environmental, social, political, economic, and corporate (Campbell, 2007; Heery et al., 2012). Such ideals have given rise to the concept of "responsible businesses" (Sharma, 2009). Democratic ideals have also played a significant role in developing the concept of responsible businesses (Sharma, 2013).

Trade unions are primarily responsible for bringing forth the voices of the labour (Pulignano, 2013), the need for their welfare (Srivastava, 2006), discourses on participatory planning as equal stakeholders to enhance conditions leading to increased productivity (Jonsson, 2007), need for better working conditions (Satrya & Parasuraman, 2007), and equitable distribution of benefits of growth (Sundar, 2007; Utting, 2007).

**National Voluntary Guidelines**

These are the guidelines which expound the social, environmental, and economic responsibilities of businesses. It was released by the Ministry of Corporate Affairs (MCA) in July 2011. Along with this the government also released a fifty eight paged white paper on this topic. The NVGs gave a set of nine principles that provides an Indian understanding and approach for inculcating responsible business conducts. It has immense role of trade unions if properly engaged with (MCA, 2011). Each clause has domains where the trade unions can be stakeholders and their views can be incorporated if strategized effectively (Baines, 2009).

The nine principles of NVGs are related to environment, public policy, inclusive growth, customers, ethics, life cycle, employees, shareholders, and human rights (MCA, 2011).

It provides meaningful opportunity for any business to operate in an economically, socially, and environmentally sustainable manner, while simultaneously balancing the demands of shareholders and other interest groups. This could be seen as a progression from non-mandatory CSR to NVG (Braithwaite, 2017). Earlier CSR was non-mandatory; however, later it was mandated at 2% of the profits. NVGs if implemented properly can enable businesses in creating value, encouraging healthy labour practices, minimizing operational risk factors, attracting and retaining customers, motivating investments and financial markets while stimulating growth.

While launching the NVG guidelines Murli Deora, the then Union Minister, Corporate Affairs, opined that India always had the concept of "parting away" with a portion of one's surplus wealth. This was done for the good of society. This is neither a modern concept nor a western import into India. The merchant has been considered as an asset from around 600 BC. They were treated with respect and civility as can be seen in ancient Indian literature like Mahabharatha and the Arthashashthra. The famous line from "Our Common Futures", report of the Bruntland Commission, was also quoted by the government. The objectives of the NVGs were to meet the "needs of the present generation without compromising on the ability of the future generations to do so" (MCA, 2011).

**Business Responsive Report**

This was a disclosure framework provided under the NVGs (MCA, 2011; Hellmann, 2013). This disclosure framework was named as the ABRR. It ensured wider evidence based uptake of the NVGs. Trade unions can play the role of assessors and maintain a form of checks and balances (Pulignano et al., 2013). Whereby, the companies cannot declare fabricated reports or exaggerated claims, which otherwise could get out of the regulatory loopholes. Such lacunae could be plugged in by effective trade union strategies.

ABRRs help in implementing the NVGs, and communicating it to the various stakeholders. It involves providing principle wise disclosures for each of the nine principles. It uses a methodology of "apply or explain". Under this methodology, companies have to give explanations as to why they could not apply any of the principles (MCA, 2011). It assists companies in re-examining its important policies and aligning them to the broader objectives of the NVGs. The vision of the NVGs and responsible businesses are fine-tuned by the ABRRs. These reports are available on the BSE and NSE websites. The top 100 listed companies have already provided these reports. This shows that successful corporations are taking the sustainability guidelines seriously, because in today's world that is only wise. It also helps in creating a customer perception which helps in the business.


**Corporate Social Responsibility**

Companies Act of 2013 mandated CSR under Clause 135. It mandated companies with "net worth of five hundred crores or more, or turnover of one thousand crore rupees or more, or a net profit of five crore rupees or more" to spend at least 2% of the "average net profits during the preceding three financial years" on CSR activities.

The Companies Act, 2013 was in itself revolutionary. Since this was the first update of India's corporate law in more than 50 years. This was passed after years of debate in the parliament. This was an attempt towards modernizing India's corporate governance rules. India was the first country to "mandate" CSR at 2% of profits. If any company fails to do so it must disclose the reasons for it.

The Act (2013) has defined CSR as activities that promote poverty alleviation programmes, educational initiatives, healthcare provisions, environmental sustainability, gender equality, and vocational skills development. Companies can decide on which area they would want to invest in. They could also alternatively contribute the amount to central or state government funds that are earmarked for socio-economic development. This definition of CSR is extremely broad and open to interpretations. It clearly emphasized corporate philanthropy rather than strategic CSR.

However, the Act does specify that the companies should try to give preference to "local areas" around which they have major operations. Trade unions can play a significant role in this by collaborating with the CSR Boards to make meaningful projects.


**Conclusion**

India, or more appropriately Bharat, since most of the gory socio-economic problems plaguing the country are overwhelmingly endemic to Bharat, has a "hungry" population of 200 million people. 50% of the women are anaemic, that translates to an absolute figure of close to 35 crore women (more than the total population of the US). Two-thirds $(2/3^{rd})$ of all Indians lack access to proper sanitation, and 400 million Indians live on less than US$ 2 a day (World Bank, 2016).

However, the paradox that has to be examined is that India is also the third largest economy in the world as per PPP. In the past two decades India has seen tremendous growth in its GDP, with an overall absolute increase of 4.5 times. The per capita consumption has increases 3 times in the same period. Similarly food grain production has increased close to 2 times; this is not considering the green revolution (Singh, 2016). But the central question that remains is how to make this growth sustainable, inclusive, equitable, and just?

The passage of the Companies Act could be hailed as a positive step forward in ensuring that businesses contribute towards creating equitable and sustainable economic development. Since, the objective was that. However, was it radical enough?

Radical enough to bring about change in this extraordinarily change averse nation characterized by its penchant for bureaucratic red-tapism? The central focus on corporate philanthropy rather than strategic sustainability has been criticized widely as a policy failure. Companies have also largely treated this "mandatory" procedure as a mere "check the box" regulatory mechanism (Dawkins, 2010; Bratihwaite, 2017).

Although, there is no shortage of organizations in India – there are an estimated 3.3 million NGOs in the country – very few have the capacity and the skills to implement any large scale impactful projects (Doh & Guay, 2004). Trade Unions can play an important role in this by identifying key project areas where projects can be implemented. This can also involve employee welfare related activities and can be incorporated under the broad spectrum of NVGs and CSR. The link between Bharat and India might lie in these crevices.

**References**

Baines, T. (2009). Integration of Corporate Social Responsibility Through International Voluntary Initiatives. *Indiana Journal of Global Legal Studies, 16*(1), 223-248.

Braithwaite, J. (2017). Types of responsiveness. In DRAHOS P. (Ed.), *Regulatory Theory: Foundations and applications* (pp. 117-132). Acton ACT, Australia: ANU Press.

Campbell, J. (2007). Why Would Corporations Behave in Socially Responsible Ways? An Institutional Theory of Corporate Social Responsibility. *The Academy of Management Review, 32*(3), 946-967.

Dawkins, C. (2010). Beyond Wages and Working Conditions: A Conceptualization of Labor Union Social Responsibility. *Journal of Business Ethics, 95*(1), 129-143.

Doh, J., & Guay, T. (2004). Globalization and Corporate Social Responsibility: How Non-Governmental Organizations Influence Labor and Environmental Codes of Conduct. *MIR: Management International Review, 44*(2), 7-29.

Epstein, E. (1989). Business Ethics, Corporate Good Citizenship and the Corporate Social Policy Process: A View from the United States. *Journal of Business Ethics, 8*(8), 583-595.

Heery, E., Williams, S., & Abbott, B. (2012). Civil society organizations and trade unions: Cooperation, conflict, indifference. *Work, Employment & Society, 26*(1), 145-160.

Hellmann-Theurer, M. (2013). Precarisation of Project Work in the Construction Industry and Trade Union Strategies for Employees' Representation. *Industrielle Beziehungen / The German Journal of Industrial Relations, 20*(2), 162-172.

Jonsson, B. (2007). Trade Union Research in Support of a Role in Development. *Indian Journal of Industrial Relations, 42*(4), 489-533.

Kleinrichert, D. (2008). Ethics, Power and Communities: Corporate Social Responsibility Revisited. *Journal of Business Ethics, 78*(3), 475-485.

Ofodile, U., Altschuller, S., Dolize, A., & Fessler, M. (2012). Corporate Social Responsibility. *The International Lawyer, 46*(1), 181-197.

Pulignano, V., Lucio, M., & Walker, S. (2013). Globalization, Restructuring and Unions: Transnational Co-ordination and Varieties of Labour Engagement. *Relations Industrielles / Industrial Relations, 68*(2), 261-289.

Satrya, A., & Parasuraman, B. (2007). Partnership as Union Strategy - Does It Work in Asia? Case Studies in Indonesia and Malaysia. *Indian Journal of Industrial Relations, 42*(4), 589-619.

Sharma, S. (2009). Corporate Social Responsibility in India: An Overview. *The International Lawyer, 43*(4), 1515-1533.

Sharma, S. (2013). Corporate Social Responsibility in India- The Emerging Discourse & Concerns. *Indian Journal of Industrial Relations, 48*(4), 582-596.

Srivastava, D. (2006). Trade Union Response to Declining Membership Base: Best Practices from Mumbai Based Trade Unions. *Indian Journal of Industrial Relations, 41*(4), 355-374.

Sundar, K. (2007). Trade Unions and Civil Society: Issues and Strategies. *Indian Journal of Industrial Relations, 42*(4), 713-734.

Utting, P. (2007). CSR and Equality. *Third World Quarterly, 28*(4), 697-712.

<u>**14th. Revisiting Keynesian theories of wage inflexibility, monetary and fiscal policies**</u>

This paper reviews the theories of money wage inflexibility as propounded by Keynes. It also studies the effects of expansionary and contractionary monetary and fiscal policies. It draws heavily from two greatly acclaimed scholarly works in this domain.

Trevithick (1976) elucidates the genesis of wage inflexibility in the Keynesian system and the appropriate labour supply function, taking explicit consideration of this. Keynesian theory of unemployment is closely related to the money wage inflexibility.

Keynes gave a central thesis that even during massive unemployment; wage rates experience downward inflexibility due to a rigid structure of "wage differentials". Historically wage bargaining has been a decentralized process whereby workers decide whether to work at below par wages or not. But because of a perceived loss of position vis-à-vis others, workers choose to be unemployed rather than work for low wages. This is in contravention to the neo-classical idea of "rational" action. In his "General Theory", Keynes accepted that the "real wage rate is equal to the marginal productivity of labour" (Trevithick, 1976). However, this does not explain the money wage rigidity after reaching the equilibrium of full employment.

The wage rate can however fall when there is a general upward swing in the level of prices, i.e. real wages will fall when the price level increases. If the wage rates are decreased due to increase in price levels, the workers are less hostile to this development. For example, suppose a worker was getting Rs. 10,000 as salary and paying a rent of Rs. 2000 and spending another Rs. 4000 on food. When the management wanted to decrease the wage rate by Rs. 500 it was met with widespread protests. So the wage level remained as is. But the rent increased by Rs. 1000 and the food prices by Rs. 500. Thus, we can see that the worker was earlier able to save Rs. 4000, now he is able to save only Rs. 2500. Although, his real wage has decreased because of this inflation in prices there were no protests or collective bargaining against this development. Keynes also argues that this rise in prices will not disturb their "relative real wage", since everyone will be affected equally, and it will also "inevitably" lead to increased employment. However, in the contemporaneous milieu this cannot be proved empirically that a rise in price level will lead to more jobs.

The concept of "money illusion" and the Hicks – Hansen IS LM model can be of use in understanding this paradox of why workers do not protest when their wages are deteriorated by price increases in lieu of direct wage cuts. This hypothesis argues that industrial relations in general, and workers in particular, are more worried about "relative real wages" than "absolute real wages", i.e. they care more about what others are earning when compared to themselves.

Zwick (1974) explains the "snapback and crowding-out" effects existing in monetary and fiscal policies. In the orthodox Keynesian IS – LM model, until commodity prices are fully adjusted, expansionary monetary policy will cause the interest rates to fall, and contractionary monetary policy will cause the interest rates to rise. This can be seen in real life examples as well, when the monetary authorities (RBI in India) lowers the interest rates so that businesses borrow in large amounts to invest and reinvigorate the economy. However, in the present context the fall in interest rates is benefitting only a miniscule section of the population who are able to exploit public money for personal gains. This is not leading to large scale industrialization that might have created jobs and which is the objective of such policies, but the funds are being siphoned off to revive the stressed assets. Moreover, excess money supply could also lead to inflationary pressures, without the adequate rise of income levels for the general populace the real wages would decrease under such conditions.

Furthermore, Zwick (1974) elucidates that initially there might be a decrease in the interest rate with expansionary policies but after a certain point it comes back to the initial stages, this has been described as the "snap-back". Same is the case with contractionary policies.

Expansionary fiscal policy leads to a rise in the levels of income, and contractionary fiscal policy leads to a fall in income. This is generally done by increasing the government spending or implementing tax cuts. There can be two primary motives behind this, first is to increase fiscal spending in order to liberate the masses from absolute abject poverty, as has been the case with schemes like MGNREGA or cash transfer subsidies, where the government tries to provide the minimum basic money for sustenance. The second motive to increase fiscal spending can be to sustain consumption and consumerist capitalism, by increasing the disposable incomes of the populace the government might indirectly try to sustain the markets by sustained consumption.

The "bond-financed government expenditure" replaces equal amounts of private spending, this has been described as "crowds out" or crowding of the expenditure market. Monetary and fiscal policy operations induce "wealth effects", "accelerator effects", and speculative "stock earning price effects". As per the "monetarists", there is an initial increase in "liquidity" as an impact effect of monetary increase; this causes the interest rates to fall. However, this is soon succeeded by the rise in incomes; this is known as "feedback effect". This again causes the interest rates to rise. "Neo-Keynesian" models use different variables to study the effects of monetary policy, but they also focus on the feedback effects by using "wealth" as a determinant of consumption.

The newer methods to explain "snapback" have continued to use the feedback effects, while the "crowding-out" has been explained using the "slope of the LM curve" or the "bond-induced shifts" of the curve. Feedback effects exist for both the monetary and fiscal policies. In practice crowding out refers to the increased government borrowing which leads to an increase in interest rates and this negatively impacts the private sector. Thus, when government spending increases through expansionary fiscal policies, it is claimed to be negatively detrimental to the private sector. However, in practice whenever the private sector faces large crises it is the government which steps in to protect the interests of the corporates, for example, after the 2008 American Financial Crisis the American government stepped in heavily to save the overall economy.

References

Trevithick, J. (1976). Money Wage Inflexibility and the Keynesian Labour Supply Function. *The Economic Journal, 86*(342), 327-332.

Zwick, B. (1974). "Snapback" and "Crowding-out" Effects in Monetary and Fiscal Policy: Explanation and Interrelation: Comment. *Journal of Money, Credit and Banking, 6*(4), 559-566.

<u>**15<sup>th</sup>. Rationality and Emotionality in organisations - A leaf from Weber**</u>

<u>List of abbreviations</u>

| | |
|---|---|
| EQ | Emotional Quotient |
| HRMS | Human Resource Management System |
| IQ | Intelligence Quotient |

<u>**Introduction**</u>

"In everything, one thing is impossible, rationality."

– Friedrich Nietzsche

It is often believed that the "rational" and "emotional" are in constant conflict. However, on punctilious contextualized engagement with the literature this can turn out to be fallacious at times. The question of emotionality at work has been one of the central concerns of sociology. Durkheim (1893) opined that division of labour leads to the fostering of positive emotions of belongingness and solidarity amongst the working groups. Marx (1896) critically challenged this argument; he put forth the theory of mechanistic commodity production leading to the generation of negative emotions, namely, anger and alienation amongst the workers. Weber (1905) predicted that with the increased rationalization, employment will become less meaningful; this will lead to the ultimate disappearance of emotions (both positive and negative) from the domain of work.

However, this theory has been critically revisited by various scholars who have contested that in reality organizations employ all possible sorts of emotional tools to bind the employees to the organization and to extract the highest possible surplus labour (Barbalet, 2000; Bandeli, 2009; Cohn, 1992; Kemper, 2004). Some such tools are mission and vision statements, orientation modules, trainings (Fulmer & Barry, 2009). The hypothesis that emotions are antithetical to the modern working organizations has undergone a critical overhaul.

Furthermore, it is important to highlight the fact that this emotionality is different from religious emotionality or religiosity (Grant et al., 2009). Extreme religiosity which was a widespread phenomenon under Catholicism and was sought to be curbed with the rise of Protestantism and capitalism is fundamentally different from the emotions that have been discussed in this paper (Hochschild, 1979). During those epochs rationality could have been considered as a revolutionary idea (Ritzger, 1975). But the incessantness, obsession, and all pervasive nature of rationality as the only guiding light of modern day organizations and society has to be examined critically.

Weber (1958) depicted bureaucracy in both private and public organizations as the "ideal-typical" model. Weberian analysis of bureaucracy also elucidates that the "disciplined, affectless, and stable" performance of responsibilities has an underlying foundational aspect of emotions, both positive and negative (Udy, 1959; Kemper, 2004).

The dichotomy between the rational and emotional has always been in existence, "Apollonian to Dionysian; Ideational to Sensate; Classical to Romantic" (Kemper, 2004). There has been a historical trend to this swing between the ideological schools of thoughts. With the advent of one doctrine and then its absolute hegemonic apogee, the other is side-lined or shunned. But this is soon followed with a failure of control complemented by sub-optimal results, this leads to the disdain for the hegemonic and ultimately the other doctrine takes apogee. This cycle is then repeated.

Weber (1968), although did not directly admire bureaucracy, he believed it to be the "most efficient and rational" path for organizing any human activity. This was the "rational-legal" authority, imperative for successful functioning of the modern world. However, he also perceived excessive rational bureaucratization as perilous for individual freedoms (Wallace, 1990). If left unregulated this heavily "rule-based, rational" bureaucracy can imprison individuals in "soulless iron cages". This could lead the world to a "glacial night of freezing darkness" (Wax, 1967).

With the collapse of the Soviet Union, and in effect the demise of Socialism or Marxism based economic organizations and polity in the early 1990s, the "market", as propounded by Adam Smith (1776) took full momentum, both in theory and praxis. The market theories and the assumptions of a "rational, self-interested" human being, "homo-economicus" (Kemper, 2004), inevitably entered the wider parlance of institutional domains. Thus, it was purported that only the market model is optimal, innovative, and rational. All societal, economic, political, and environmental decisions were taken accordingly. Thus, almost in all such instance the roles for emotions was completely omitted and expunged. They were only considered as noises or disturbances to the wider organizational objectives.

Weber in his famous book, *Economy and Society* (published posthumously in 1968), gives the example of stock exchange panics and military campaigns. He goes to the extent of declaring emotions as irrational factors. These are antagonistic to the rational factors and if not properly eliminated might deter the proper establishment of causal relationships. According to him a well-developed bureaucracy is characterized by "*sine ira ac studio*" (absence of passion or bias). This also laid the groundwork for making a "dehumanized" bureaucracy. This is extremely problematic since rationality is thus viewed as interlinked with the lack of basic human ideals of love, care, and mutual wellbeing.

Another important aspect is of social action and the idea of "Affektuel" – emotions. This is of particular importance because during the period of Weberian writings the social impact of businesses were of the least concern to the capitalists (Weyher, 2012). However, the contemporary contexts are absolutely dissimilar. Sustainability – economic, political, environmental, and corporate are of prime significance. Thus, irrational factors – like emotions, play an increasingly important role in defining what is rational.

## Part II - Emotionlessness

However, the idea of emotionlessness of organizations cannot be completely disparaged and dismissed. Being unbiased also means that organization and institutions in the public and private domains will be able to perform in an equitable manner without giving undue advantages to anyone. If the idea of rationality is upheld in the true spirit, it has many positively reinforcing reverberations (Seo & Barret, 2007).

According to Weberian analysis, complete emotionlessness cannot be practiced in actuality, but is nevertheless one of the key components of the "ideal type" of organization or bureaucracy. A fully developed organization will have functionaries with impersonal and mechanized activities. These functionaries or bureaucrats, as per Weber, will only look at the development of the organization without any emotions (Barbalet, 2000). But this in itself is paradoxical, since any human who will work for an organization with utmost sincerity will have to believe in its ideals, mission, and vision. Thus, in essence this functionary is actually emotionally involved with the organization. This emotional involvement was completely neglected by Weber and many subsequent scholars. Even the most rational organizations have to generate emotions in their employees to enable them in participating optimally in the production activities.

Weber (1905) also claims that the religious notions of eternal salvation could be specifically linked to the development of entrepreneurship and capitalism. These religious ideals actually generated the emotion of anxiety which was closely linked to the subsequent economic actions. The argument for emotionlessness is also soaked in duality. For bureaucrats functioning in organizations this duality is exemplified in two categorical differentiations. First, the clients or the governed, for them the bureaucrat (or the organization) has to maintain complete emotionlessness. Second, the structural superiors, like the master or chief, they must evoke an emotion of respect. This duality can be found in modern day organizations as well. The customers and employees are actually the governed, who are at the bottom of the pyramid. They are dealt with the least of regard. But, the owners and major shareholders wield considerable power and reap all the benefits of the organization. The "collectivist organization" was proposed as an alternative to the traditional rational-bureaucratic models (Rothschil-Whitt, 1979). In the Indian context some successful examples of this could be found in the dairy cooperatives across various states.


## Part III - Organizations and intrinsic emotions

Considering the aspect of employment in organizations, although it is claimed that to be disciplined and rational while working, one must be emotionless. However, the core matter in this regard is the issue of job security. If an individual who is employed by an organization is rational and disciplined it ensures his job security, which in itself leads to the arousal of emotions like a sense of overall security and wellbeing. Weber (1958) further explains this point using the concepts of "tenure for life" and social security benefits provided by the organizations to its employees by means of pension. All this proves that employment is not a "null state emotion" as has been claimed, but it has a positive emotional arousal, the feel good factors (Smith-Lovin, 1989; Kemper, 2004).

Positions of power also have an emotional undertone to them. When one feels powerful they experience a sense of autonomy and security, thus power is also inherently linked to emotions (Weber, 1968; Udy, 1959). Attainment of power is closely linked to achievement of these emotional senses. Modern organizations have been able to brilliantly exploit this by ensuring a disciplined conformity among their employees using a quid pro quo arrangement. Wherein, they have to exert the power positions in order to experience the emotions attached therewith. This also leads to the successful perpetuation of structural hierarchies.

Organizations both in the public and private sector thrive by providing its bureaucrats (or employees) with positions that give "status honour" and "social esteem" (Weber, 1968; Kemper, 2004). These are interlinked with a specific lifestyle, perks, benefits, and certain social privileges that are part of the package. It creates various social classes and restrictions on "social intercourse". These are very important for the maintenance of order in the society by the organizations using its bureaucrats. The bureaucrats in return get emotional gratification by feeling a sense of satisfaction, happiness, and pleasure. This is very evident in the contemporary society as well where the top management executives or the government officials ("babus") maintain an elitist social stratification, often known as "babudom" or bureaucratic officialdom. The attainment of certain educational certificates is often seen as the gateways to entry to these elite social circles in the organizations. The feeling of being superior to others in a social system is itself an emotional experience, both for the superior and the inferior. Thus, organizations successfully use these emotional bases to maintain their operations, the social classes and their reproduction. When others submit to these bureaucrats, they feel a sense of superiority and social accomplishment over these "others", which helps in the continuation of the system and the organization. Even if the submission by the "governed" is coerced, they make sure that it is not visible to the bureaucrats, it must be perceived as authentic. Otherwise it might be negatively detrimental to them (Wallace, 1990; Kemper, 2004).

These sentiments of superiority in the bureaucrats also help in the enforcement of the rational-legal objectives of the organization. Since this is accompanied with the development of a sense of general disdain and contempt for the governed, the bureaucrat is at comfort while implementing even the ghastliest of norms on the governed. This helps the bureaucrats by sparing them any feelings of guilt or shame, and again is beneficial for the organizations. The scope for the existence of any compassion is completely eliminated.

Objective imperturbability of officials in an organization is developed by using the means of symbolic idealisms, either to charismatic leaders (or owners) or to societal values. Loyalty is an important component of this. It is exemplified by loyalty to an office rather than a person. Many great institutions have sustained because of this. However, what merits our attention is that loyalty in itself is a coalescence of various emotions. It involves "Wertrational" (value based) actions that are directly contradictory to the "Zweckrational" (purely rational) actions (Weber, 1950). Organizations exploit this concept of loyalty by obscuring the individuals and directing it towards the organization.

Apart from the positive emotions of security, satisfaction, and loyalty, there exists another negative emotion which is successfully utilized by organizations to control its employees – fear. This emotion is wielded by the tool of "appointment to office" (Weber, 1968). The employees who do not conform to discipline can be remitted out of office. Since most of the employees are appointed and paid salaries along with recommendations, promotions, pension, and social security by the organizations, they fear losing all these benefits of office. The organization becomes more powerful, creating a power deficit and dependence. This generates fear. The bureaucrats in the higher echelons of the structure can use this fear component to utilize the employees as per their perusal. This is particularly true for formal undemocratic organizations.

Scrutinizing the case of uniforms one can determine the notion of emotionality attached in essence. Uniforms are used for military, police, etc. This provides organizations to utilize uniforms as multifarious tools for emotional repertoire. It generates the feelings of camaraderie, solidarity, nationality, and pride. Also, whenever there is any defeat the emotions of shame and despair are stimulated (Weber, 1958).

## Conclusion

Thus, on careful examination of the rationality – emotionality dichotomy, one can conclude that the ideal-typical archetype of a bureaucrat in an organization can only be successfully achieved by employing automatons (or robots) and not human beings. Since, no human can truly be emotionless. The emotions are being used to bind the employees to the organization. It is ironical that rationality is being used as an excuse to "dehumanize" employees by expediting its emotionality towards the organization.

Nath (2011) conducted a study in which 77 offshored call center employees were interviewed. This study is of importance to the current paper because of the emotional labour that was attached to these jobs. The employees were subjected to various emotional ordeals which were institutionalized in the organizations by the means of "national identity management". This shows that although organizations would want to profess rationality as a concept, when it comes to actual practice, it will not shy away from exposing its employees to emotionally tormenting situations.

The inherent emotionality of the employees is also being engineered by the organizations to increase productivity and profitability. For example, giving services with a smile, care giving professions like nursing have been closely interlinked with emotional labour put in by the nurses. Theories by Mayo (1945) and Maslow (1958) have forced organizations to develop the human relations models of management to efficiently deal with the emotionality of labour. These models have also linked intrinsic rewards from employment (leading to emotional fulfilment) and productivity gains. This practice has been further popularized in the contemporaneous organizational milieus where the knowledge workers are being increasingly deputed to roles which align with their internal value systems. This ensures the employees will put in their "hearts and souls" into client servicing. Newer forms of emotive management approaches have also been developed by organizations, like the "bounded emotionality" model (Martin et al., 1998).

With the increasing "commercialization of feelings" (Hochschild, 2003), the organizations are faced with a multitude of ethical dilemmas (Fulmer & Barry, 2009). Furthermore, with the advent of various computerised management information systems (MIS) a lot of organizational functions are being computerized leaving very little scope for exercise of emotionality (Argyris, 1971). This can be seen with the introduction of human resource management system (HRMS) software in various companies. Thus, organizations are at critical crossroads of organizational development and management theory development. The paradigm is undergoing a rapid change. All the contours of traditional organizations both in formal and informal sectors are undergoing swift changes. With the development of concepts like EQ complementing IQ, emotionality is no longer an inferior quality at work. The traditional concepts of ideal-typical bureaucratic organizations have to adapt to contemporaneous changes to be of relevance and to be successful in the markets. Even historically, as has been detailed in the paper, emotions were never out of the ambit of organizations. In fact they were used for the benefit of the organizations to control the employees in the multifarious ways. Thus, it can be concluded that rationality and emotionality are closely interlinked. They can exist in complement to each other and have been utilized by organizations for their survival and profiteering.

<u>**References**</u>

Argyris, C. (1971). Management Information Systems: The Challenge to Rationality and Emotionality. *Management Science,17*(6), B275-B292.

Bandelj, N. (2009). Emotions in Economic Action and Interaction.*Theory and Society, 38*(4), 347-366.

Barbalet, J. (2000). "Beruf", rationality and emotion in max weber's sociology. *European Journal of Sociology / Archives Européennes De Sociologie / Europäisches Archiv Für Soziologie, 41*(2), 329-351.

Cohn, S. (1992). Class differences in emotionality: implications of cognitive theories. *Humboldt Journal of Social Relations, 18*(2), 1-23.

Durkheim, E´mile. (1893) . *The Division of Labor in Society*. New York: Free Press.

Fulmer, I., & Barry, B. (2009). Managed Hearts and Wallets: Ethical Issues in Emotional Influence by and within Organizations.*Business Ethics Quarterly, 19*(2), 155-191.

Grant, D., Morales, A., & Sallaz, J. (2009). Pathways to Meaning: A New Approach to Studying Emotions at Work. *American Journal of Sociology, 115*(2), 327-364.

Hochschild, A. (1979). Emotion work, feeling rules, and social structure. American Journal of Sociology, 85: 551-75.

Hochschild, A. (2003). The managed heart: Commercialization of feeling. Berkeley: University of California Press.

Kemper, T. (2004). The differential impact of emotions on rational schemes of social organization: reading weber and coleman, in J.H. Turner (Ed.)*Theory and Research on Human Emotions (Advances in Group Processes) (*pp. 223 – 244). USA: Emerald Group Publishing Limited.

Martin, J., Knopoff, K., & Beckman, C. (1998). An Alternative to Bureaucratic Impersonality and Emotional Labor: Bounded Emotionality at The Body Shop. *Administrative Science Quarterly,43*(2), 429-469.

Marx, K. (1896) (1906). Das Capital, vol. 1. New York: International.

Maslow, A. 1958. *Motivation and Personality*. New York: Harper & Row.

Mayo, E. 1945. *The Social Problems of an Industrial Civilization*. Boston: Harvard University, Graduate School of Business Administration.

Mody, M., Day, J., Sydnor, S. & Jaffe, W. (2016). Examining the motivations

NASSCOM. (2007). Catalyzing Change. New Delhi: NASSCOM Foundation.

Nath, V. (2011). Aesthetic and emotional labour through stigma: National identity management and racial abuse in offshored Indian call centres. *Work, Employment &*

*Society, 25*(4), 709-725.

Ritzer, G. (1975). Professionalization, Bureaucratization and Rationalization: The Views of Max Weber. *Social Forces, 53*(4), 627-634.

Rothschild-Whitt, J. (1979). The Collectivist Organization: An Alternative to Rational-Bureaucratic Models. *American Sociological Review, 44*(4), 509-527.

Seo, M., & Barrett, L. (2007). Being Emotional during Decision Making: Good or Bad? An Empirical Investigation. *The Academy of Management Journal, 50*(4), 923-940.

Smith, A. (1776). *An Inquiry into the Nature and Causes of the Wealth of Nations*. Edwin Cannan, ed. 1904. Library of Economics and Liberty.

Smith-Lovin, L. (1989). Sentiment, Affect, and Emotion. *Social Psychology Quarterly, 52*(1), V-Xii.

Udy, S. (1959). "Bureaucracy" and "Rationality" in Weber's Organization Theory: An Empirical Study. *American Sociological Review, 24*(6), 791-795.

Wallace, W. (1990). Rationality, Human Nature, and Society in Weber's Theory. *Theory and Society, 19*(2), 199-223.

Wax, M. (1967). Magic, rationality, and Max Weber. *The Kansas Journal of Sociology, 3*(1), 12-19.

Weber, M. (1950). The social causes of the decay of ancient civilization. *The Journal of General Education,5*(1), 75-88.

Weber, M. (1958). *From max weber: Essays in sociology*. In: H. Gerth & C. Wright Mills (Trans. and

Weber, M. (1958). Science as a Vocation. *Daedalus, 87*(1), 111-134.

Weber, M. (1968). *Economy and society*. Berkeley: University of California Press.

Weber, M. (1981). Some Categories of Interpretive Sociology. *The Sociological Quarterly, 22*(2), 151-180.

Weber, M. (1905) 1958. *The Protestant Ethic and the Spirit of Capitalism*. New York: Charles Scribner.

Weyher, L. (2012). Re-reading Sociology via the Emotions: Karl Marx's Theory of Human Nature and Estrangement.*Sociological Perspectives, 55*(2), 341-363.